AUTHORS DIGITAL ENTERPRISE

A MASTER GUIDE FOR AMAZON BOOKSELLERS

BY MALINI CHAUDHRI Ph.D.

AUTHORS DIGITAL ENTERPRISE.   MAINI CHAUDHRI

AUTHORS DIGITAL ENTERPRISE.   MAINI CHAUDHRI

INTRODUCTION

Center for Wellness is a Skills development knowledge provider, developed under the auspices of ISTE, and bears statutes to carry out its assignments. It was proposed in 2010 to support a new era of technical and certified digital learning in spa therapy skills and related competencies based on Occupational Standards.

The founder author, Malini Chaudhri. Ph.D. L.Ac (WHO. China), discovered a niche market in authoring in this time whilst digital disruption precipitated changes in Education. The rise of artificial intelligence and automation caused further need for deep work. Her social networks and feeds adjusted to the changes in the Internet calling for increased robotic support and neural learning.

Since 2016, she followed the deeper structures of the Internet in business which impacted the internet and the field. Her association with Amazon and many authoring styles, continued to evolve into the new modern idiom and language of the digital era. The B2B marketplace, Angel investor's platform, blogs, social streams, apps and LMS sites, merged into a new significant reality, where all of a sudden, everything had concluded, yet everything remained. Now change was possible as far as we consciously moved the motion into the artificial space.

The founder, author is associated with a dynamic and disruptive past experience, she has supported companies, on the verge of collapsing, to turnaround and influence the field as leaders. Her career evolved despite great circumstantial opposition and disruption, where her country was not aligned to the seals of the task. In ISTE she found great solace and support in the senior academic handling of process and change and integration with policy makers. The continuing revolution, however, challenged absolutely everywhere and all sustainable development.

This Guide from Malini Chaudhri is associated with her works in her blog on Amazon Central, and her technical management of listings for her Center, regulated by ISTE, which has been committed to deep work and deep learning as it must be arranged for authors to mobilize their lot into digital citizenship. Her professional experience and example has indicated prominence and relevance, only through technical identification of issues facing the business, and listings of the same, in order that audits and Quality Assurance is possible. All this with the knowledge that Google has a disruptive role in the system. Disruption, change and conflict is very high in the new landscape.

The role of competition assessment, the tactics managed for survival, the strategies for minimizing conflict, the in depth management of Time through automation, the significance of metrics to present Big Data, the focus on shareholders and the location of funds, has shifted the mind-set of the author towards a new spectrum.

Yet in this Author, the logic of the past remains. Technical Standards, basics for regulatory boards and authors guilds, for law offices and statutes, for achievement based on humane practise, social welfare and ethics is merit more than metrics and monetary controls. There is scope for predictive analysis, without direct confrontation of impossible reasoning and chaotic working relationships across the globe from some of the the uncontrolled development of IOT.

This Author, has comfort in the ideology and literacy of other authors and her kind that troubleshoot, and convey the imbalance of the world in its situations and development in acceptable idioms.

ABOUT THE AUTHOR

Malini Chaudhri is an author with privileges and statutes of four books on alternative medicine and spa sciences. She is a life member of ISTE with authorization to provide skills globally. This license supports structured assessments and forecasts at national level of development.

She has embraced change and continued to make an impact on her professional field through top level research and publication.
She has attended seminars and courses worldwide, and managed two International Qualifications, one belonging to UK Ministry in India.
She has lived in China, USA and India

Her projects cover branches of spa therapies and alternative medicine.
Her authors works cover technical data and competencies for careers.

She teaches courses on Eliademy.
She has interests in law and manages to progress through rigorous enforcement of judicial standards in social, professional and personal issues.

ACKNOWLEDGEMENTS

I express my appreciation and gratitude for all the experts who sent me support through Push notifications, whilst I was struggling to find data for this book.

I thank Get Response, AWeber, Webgility, Kapost, Curata, Typeform, Hubspot, Leanplum, Splitly, Jumpsend, Salesforce, Amazon, Facebook, Ingram Spark, Netline Portal, Apex, Bitrix24.com amongst the many supporting content providers aiding the 2017 digital revolution.

Quote

"Content Marketing is a strategic marketing approach focused on creating and distributing valuable, relevant, and consistent content to attract and retain a clearly-defined audience—and, ultimately, to drive profitable customer action."

Content Marketing Institute

CONTENTS

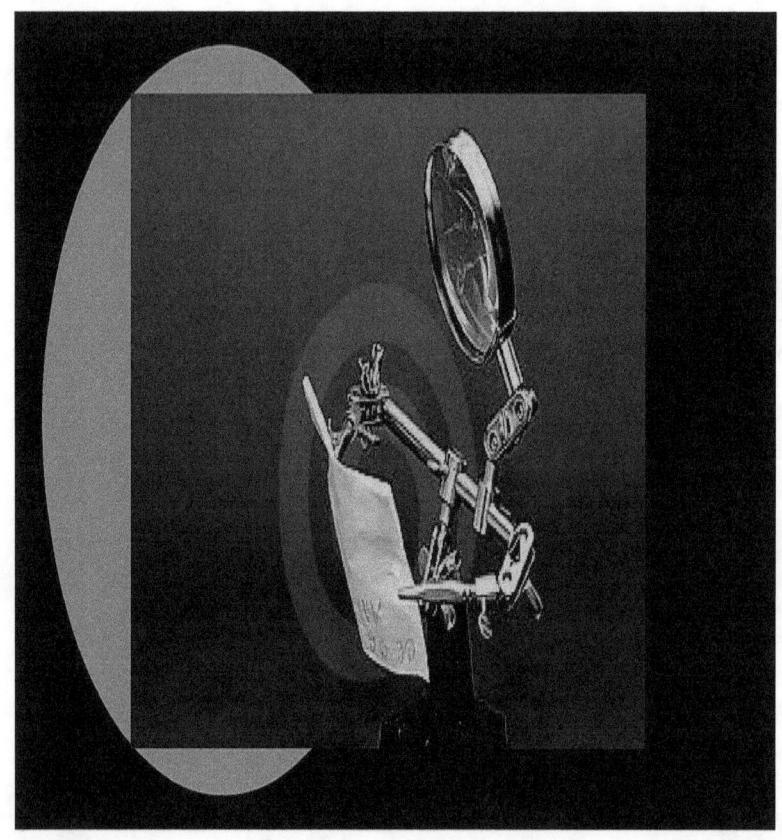

AMAZON AND THE READERS MARKET PLACE

Since 2017 March, the internet changed historically. Amazon has been a major player in its structure to develop the B2Band B2C marketplace. Algorithm changes and core developments influencing the internet's deepest structures were further incorporated. The Amazon factor critically influenced how the internet would shape up for buyers and sellers, to arrange a professional digital landscape. By now many other world markets had closed and jobs were giving way to affiliate sales or first party sellers.

Amazons technical advantage has been rooted in its robotic laboratories, where machine learning and programming have been inducted. The intensive structured organization based on ASIN, and ISBN, organized products, sellers and books into metadata marked digital entities that moved on the internet. For authors, this marketplace has been arranged to the deepest alignment of digital presence possible till now in the world. The author has secured his identity, his movement, his readers, fans, critics, newsmakers, subject experts, fellow authors and much more into a very exceptional database. More than that in his working lifetime, his product (book) continues to move in the arena, based on conscious inputs and seller techniques. There are associated Amazon companies for authors as Good reads and Create space, Author Central, Kindle Boards, and a host of Amazon affiliates with different promotional schemes. This is in addition to inbuilt campaign support for advertisers.

Reviews, five star ratings, traffic, visits to book, sale scans, buyer locations, and currencies can provide author and sales ranks in the larger picture, thereby giving big data. These are very advanced technical, integrated, mechanisms at work. Implementation to some extent of language translations, shows alignment with Deep Learning. Generally all cataloguing and support provided, have a deeper impact on the internet, if the seller is Amazon listed than if not. An author's blog in any Amazon site is deeper located than one not on Amazon, if the author can manage complete optimization within its technical apparatus. Optimization is a very broad concept and authors will locate a comfortable threshold from which to grow.

Since March 2017, the UI (User Experience), has become an important part of the system. By now programmed robotics are giving users support to follow their choice and have a very responsive experience in the marketplace. Their identities, choices, browsing, location, spending patterns and their related activities on the internet, become a digital footprint. Sellers are dependent on this to keep the marketplace boosted and their products with accelerated sales, data tracking and CRM. Of late integrations into the new packages to boost sales is available for Amazon sellers of the marketplace. These are expensive opportunities for sellers to control their own data and performance in the marketplace. These apps belong to the new internet and required standard of deep work from authors.

Jungle Scout :

This an app which can be used to scale Amazons vast marketplace and obtain information on its products. It helps Amazon sellers avoid failure and have access to the big data. Vendors based on enterprise with exhaustive data research, benefit from this app.

Fetcher:

This a modern accounting software for Amazon sellers. It fetches data, provides advanced business analytics which support sale strategies. This app supports Fintech and robotic based AI.

Splitly:

This a popular app used for product list optimization and continued seller advancement in the marketplace. It split tests images and texts, and pricing. For great outreach, competitive markets and accelerated web traffic, this deep system is essential support.

Webgility:

This integration reflects the blueprint for the new e-commerce market. Excel sheets and manual entries must be replaced by automation and integration. Online sellers in the face of increasing traffic and competition, will take control of their own work flow.
These are amongst a few of the recommended systems available in the new automated apparatus. Many other integrations may also support CRM and data tracking. Vendors can find a suitable arrangement.

Feedly:

This a popular site which may be subscribed to with integrations specifically for authors and for content sharing? Feedly vault provides free and paid integration for working teams through SLACK (slack also manages further integration), **IIITF** (with integrations to Amazons Alexa, Facebook, messaging, email and Microsoft office. **Slack** has advanced Messenger Slackbot support for users and teams, Paperbot for recognizing visitors and optimizing and several hundred high tech integrations. Feedly is important as a supporting newsite to provide the user with updated content relevant to his profile, browsing, reading, and current interests through keywords and categories.

Kapost:

 Kapost is an example of an independent B2B marketing operating system on Cloud with forty integrations that enables content marketers to manage the marketing function amid the complexity of the digital age. Kapost aligns the organization's teams, tools and channels, to enable the user to effectively execute, distribute and analyse content across the buyer's journey. It is for large scale operations and workforce. Kapost is an alternative solution for Authors Enterprise to Amazon (difference and metadata values excluded).

Kapost has vast free resources on B2B marketplace operations, and offers free downloads of templates for crowd funding, and micro operations in workflow.

Slack:

Integrations authors to arrange their own sellers platform and enterprise structures. Slack is an immensely advanced platform for artificial Intelligence and machine based support where teams require training, collaboration and secure content building. It is a perfect platform for work teams and has several hundred popular apps as Github, Zendesk, and Lever to manage volume scaling.

Authors are also advised to develop integrations or rely on bots that support data tracking. This is because the new internet is permitting many new layers of information to be visible. Licensed companies can sell off data on the author's credit cards, their contacts, their key buyers and supporters, and trade of information to competitors in minutes. The author should have an integrated platform which identifies if a User is good or bad. The Internet can decipher this. In brief the business situation is not private as we are used to it.

In case a User shows a suspicious tracking, the author can report to local cyber police, Amazon support, and to sites as Facebook Live. The internet will have a provision to confirm the authors report status and clear the issue. However the author must be well programmed in his reporting, manage screenshots, details, proof, and precise facts, in case the helpline fails to respond and further investigations are necessary. The author can identify anonymous users, and differentiate from hackers. Many users must be converted to fans and buyers with good responsiveness to the authors books on Amazon.

At any rate, UI and Data tracking are the new focus of the seller, based on the deep systems. Additional new apparatus includes, video marketing and email marketing to woo the User and support his experience. Data may be monitored and enterprise scaled as in the case of rate of conversion, opened emails, responsive users, clicks and purchases. Email typography, colour, mood, language style should be branded for the internet to pick up the digital stamp of the Vendor.

A new system that has emerged to control vulnerable financial and business data, is **Influencer marketing**. Amazon is now launching this system. Influencers will provide connectivity for vendors to move in the internet securely, and rivals or thieves can be detected. **Linkis.com**, for instance, is a twitter site which boosts visibility of author's links in close connection to Bill Gates network. Other influencers in the network may patrol sites, moderate or recommend. These Influencers must be acknowledged for their immense support to secure good users in the social sites. Expert Influencers and moderators have boosted many individuals working hard on the internet and stabilized the transition in association with Intellisystems.it. Jeff Bezos portals may be subscribed to in addition with Amazons. Mark Zuckerberg has influencer significance for developers on Facebook and new incoming technologies, cameras and range of internet programmed intelligence. Satellite supporting technologies that move the internet, are linked to advanced robotic networks and laboratories, and there commercial figureheads.

All aspects of the internet must be compact, integrated, secure and analysed. All aspects are formal, including CTA, optimization and detail, email secure integration and connectivity, vendor marketplace graphics, images, typography, pricing, category and keywords and essential plugins for personalized sales.

Other popular choices for Amazon book sellers include:

Word Press and Drupal– A comprehensive website builder, with multiple theme designs and plugin options for shopping carts (i.e. Woo Commerce).

Big Cartel – Builds a unique online store with customized colours, fonts, and colours.

Gum road - An online store with simple setup, support features, and analytics. Aimed toward creators and artists.

Selz and Facebook pages. – Create online stores or sell via social. They have multiple themes to choose from and built-in payments.

Shopify and Kartrocket– An e-commerce platform that allows the seller to build a store within their platform. Rich with features and tools.

These are only a few in the list for small scale enterprise

Marketplace with tools for scaling

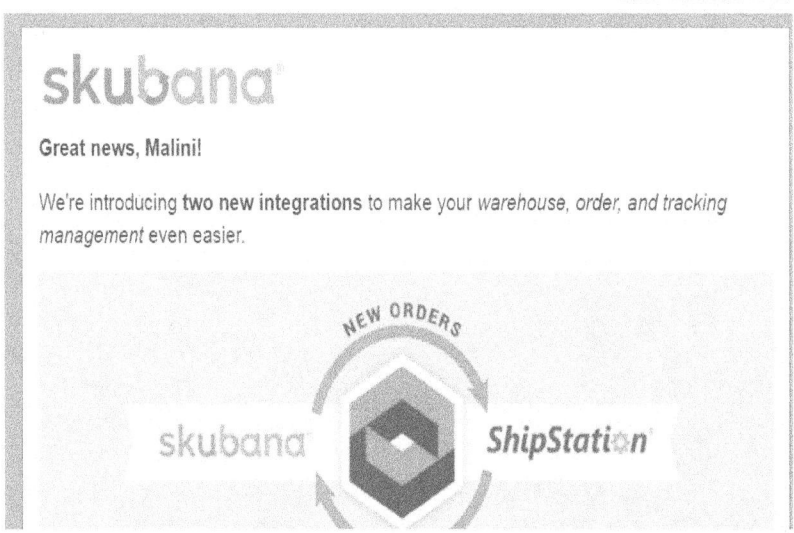

Skubana and ShipStation.
Terapeak
Scribed
Jumpsend
Just Uno
Klaviyo
Help Scout
Workato
Netline Portal
Get Response

The latest technologies are based on synchronized communications that are personalized and elite. Appropriate customers are informed through webinars, videos and eBooks of their systems.

THE HEART GROWS FONDER. Express emotions, moods and personality on the internet. The internet will keep you pleased. The new internet generates social and AI based footprints for the marketplace. Invite readers to express through emoji

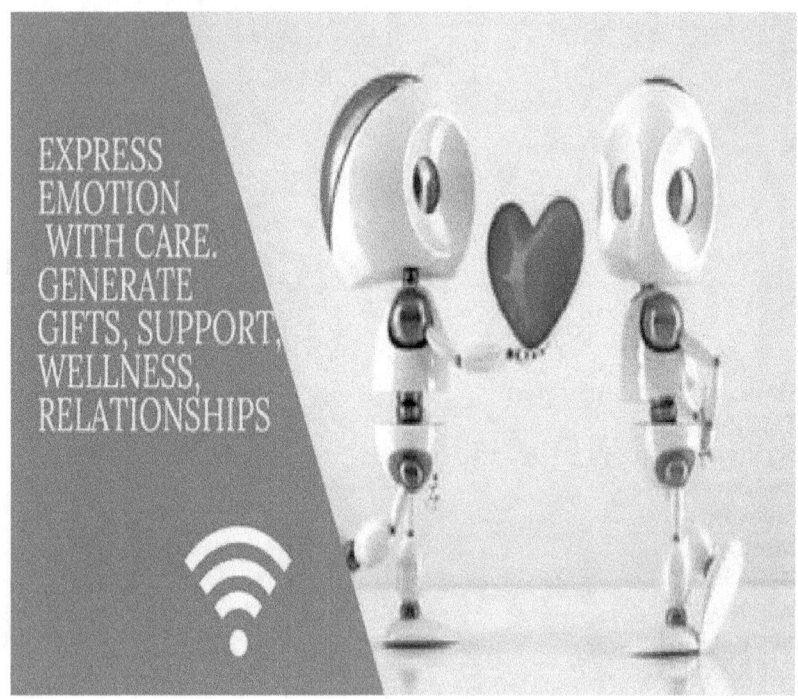

AUTHORS NEW INTERNET

Since March 2017, the predictability of search engines has wavered. Changes are not deciphered or applied easily. Preferred engines as Google and Bing have become skill specific. The Google systems employ Algorithm updates and methods of page rank, that have SEO preferences that guide the spider to move to prominence on the web. Keyword cluttering, repetitions, bad images, bad chats, bad websites, porn, plagiarism, hacking and immature tactics have been rejected. Mobile networks, maps, integrated brand links amongst other features improves visibility on search engines. However the new sciences of SEO are less understood and the impact of unskilled users is high. The Google satellite gives enhanced views of roads, people, earthquake disaster relief and ecosystems. It activates another system based on geo-location, city life, internet automated controls and safety process. However the same sensitive data reception systems can be intrusive in authors IP and data, in emails, passwords and conversations. The differences are known to trouble unprepared Influencers of the internet.

The legal, documented policies of all key players are not interactive or integrated. The engine often crashes competitor sites as Amazon. Google Plus rejects visitors. So does Gmail. Google maps have powerful satellite visibility, and geo location search is avoided when threats or trailing in physical space is anticipated. It seems that Google caters to a community of professionals that understand internet language, and mechanisms to control web visitors. This means that user skills are needed to be boosted in order to perform well on Google.

Important search engines available outside of Google and Bing for authors includes Opera, Mozilla Firefox, Yandex, Safari, Chinese browsers, and Ask.com. In addition, experts recommend Search Engine Land as a search site that has configured updates in engine performance and has processed the new machinery. Webmaster World is another search engine based on advanced updates for marketers. Search Engine Watch is also an approved search engine for businesses and assessment of company sites, restaurants, roads, traffic and related information. Browsers have to be multilingual, with translation features, and security controls.

 Authors can assess their browsers and accompanying extensions, apps, browser security add-ons, themes, synchronized emails, and engine styles. In brief, the search engine algorithm changes that authors must know include

1) Accelerated Mobile Pages (AMP). AMP has become a phenomenon in the SEO community for it allows consumers load pages instantly at a reduced data rate. SEO is high with mobile integration for authors. Instagram scores provide higher ratios for any activity than Facebook or Twitter.

2) Artificial Intelligence. Search Engines have employed artificial Intelligence, to give the most relevant information in a prioritized system for the user. User friendly landing pages, and Info graphics supports this feature for website navigation.

 3) Personal branding. Branded urls, well defined sites, and integrated branded links can support visibility. Fortune 500 companies as Pepsi, NY Times, have experienced 35% increase in CTR based on branded links. Some important SEO updates are No Multiple Pages with the Same Keyword are necessary Get Rid of Auto-generated Content and Roundup/Comparison Type of Pages

*Pages with 1-2 Paragraphs of Text Only are not processed.
*The Internet likes New Content
*Be Careful with Affiliate Links and Ads
*Too Many Outbound Links with Keywords are bad.
 *Geo Location Matters Over-Optimization of Website is not necessary.
*Strong Domains Matter
*The Top Heavy Update: Pages with Too Many Ads above the Fold Now Penalized by Google's "Page Layout" Algorithm. This keeping in mind, that Customer Experience is priority on the internet systems, and generates automated support, whereas advertisements bring in predetermined, non-digital data.

The Internet is based on supporting machine learning with Artificial Intelligence, bots, emoji's and giphy's. It has been rearranged with Deep Learning systems, automated translations across the world, neural networks that support coping and adapting to the internet language. It has given impetus to new prolific apps, and scope of advanced metrics or feedback scales.

Other listings relevant to the new internet as presented by W3 Techs are listed below:
Server side programming languages include
 PHP
ASP.NET
 JAVA
STATIC FILES
COLD FUSION

Client side programming languages
JAVASCRIPT
FLASH
SILVERLIGHT

 Most popular web servers for developers and technicians include
APACHE
NGINX
 MICROSOFT
IIS LITESPEED
 GOOGLE SERVERS

MESSENGER, BOTS, CAMERA, LIVE VIDEO STORIES, CHAT, MAIL, NOTES, CALENDAR, GEO-
LOCATION
THE NEW FACE OF AUTOMATION FOR THE AUTHOR

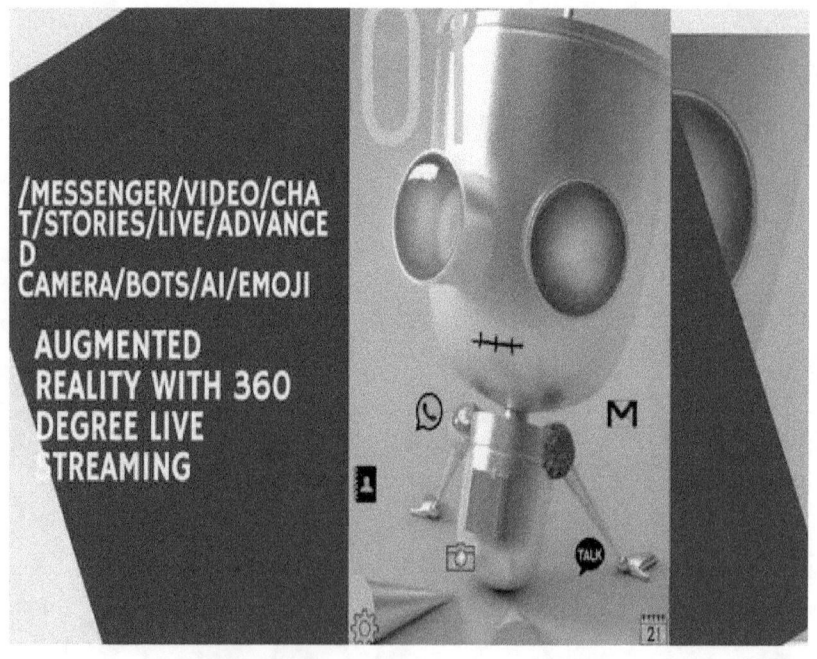

THE AUTHOR AND AUTOMATION

The author has now entered the era of automation, where the tools at hand and enterprise process is more advanced, strategic and highly organized than ever before. Artificial Intelligence algorithms have reformulated the industry, and prioritized, disciplined and reinforced process of workflow, style, technique, social and rank in a new continuum. The process now available must be recognized and assembled for authors own use, industry and community, based on the automated inbuilt new support structure.

The shift is not too hard, as there are robotics available that are seen on the internet as 'ASSISTANT', 'Intelligence Agent' , 'Guide', 'Consultant' or similar. Advanced support may come through cloud solutions or new updates. Key automation belong to GAF (Google, Amazon, and Facebook). Google has Allo. Amazon has Alexa. Facebook has Emoji and Live Video to support fast and relevant information technology. This is to list just a few of the systems arranged. Many platforms emerging will continue to offer support via chat bots. These are robotic configurations that assess authors' needs as they work. Chat bots, group bots, personal bots and many others may pop up on the screen to offer advice.

Changes incorporated have strategically promoted the best user experience possible for developing books. Data scientists discovered the use of dataset to give added responsiveness and advantage in the system. Machine learning for the author, automation, and structured sophistication continue to smoothen out workflow process that gives relevance to the Internet of Things.

ASSISTANT Amazon Assistants as Alexa, Apple's Siri, and Cortana can capacitate and enable skills for performing moderately complex tasks. Artificial Intelligence can support through voice or message, through indirect screen freezes, through arrows to alternative information process that completes the task at hand. Posts, or emails for instance, may have sound enablement that support User experience on the browser.

Major Internet market players have emerged simultaneously with the sound bot that speeds up the shift to a future work process.

GUIDES Another level of robotics may be noted in Guides, which offer directions, point at issues or irregularities. In a cockpit of a flight, in dense clouds, the Guide is activated to steer the vessel towards safety. Authors would use Guides if inviting the user to give a review or rate the book in a large community, where steering may be needed.

CONSULTANT Consultant bots give differential diagnosis and support with rationale. A site may notice too frequent shares, and activate a consultant to advise not to return. Russian social sharing sites have this bot. In fact the robotics has already interpreted that the data exists in their site from a prior time, and further shares will be rejected. OK.RU asks customers to leave if they have shared a post before. This may be simply a message, a image or a chat in other channels.

COLLEAGUE A colleague will help enterprise and offer data centric solutions to move tasks, cash flow, work flow. An AI colleague might recommend referencing and/or attaching a presentation in an email; This bot analyses bigger enterprise data, and supports the customer experience through updated technological complex process. The internet analyses emails, language, mood, style, and configuration of email recipients. Many tasks get reorganized by the automated technical inbuilt software. Authors may develop skills to use these bots in personalized treatments for conversation, engagement, lead generation, B2B marketplace swales and much more.

BOSS Where colleagues and consultants advise, bosses direct. Boss AI is designed for obedience and compliance; the human surrenders to the algorithm in the system. It demands extreme precision, timing, instruction and scope for secure enterprise operations. Disaster management, police signalling, earthquake rescues are examples of events that are based on AI Boss controls. Boss bots will be useful for

Authors who develop highly integrated technical portals of workflow. CRM, analytics, breakdowns, security updates and related are offered from Boss bots. Bots may be conversational, or nonverbal, simply based on signs or smileys. They may have a character, appearance as a cartoon, a name or may be smiley. In any case they are effective robot signal systems that decipher the user and provide strong support. Engagement and responsiveness is enhanced. Inbuilt automation of bots, may be based on data of prior trends of customers, their emotional and psychological level, and typically provide systematic attributes to engage specific personalities in users. The comfort zone of the customer should improve in the environment from the assistant robot.

Authors will learn to locate supporting systems embedded in the internet to cater to personal needs. Bots grow smarter the more they are interacted with. The scope of support is far more intensive than possible from human factors. The machine must become a companion to enhance skills and connectivity.

The scope of artificial intelligence via bots and author supports, visibility in search engines, ranks and ratings, rests around the authors ability to manipulate crucial keywords in his word, and to keep them optimized through the methods listed in this book.

The author may use keywords in the two layers of the page,

- a) The Content
- b) The metadata

At both levels the keywords may be contained in the

*title,
*subtitle,
*content,
*tag,
* Image
And may also be optimized against the authors profile skills in his LinkedIn page, Xing page other. Keywords should be professionally located. Authors can use support of tools

available.

The Next Web

TNW

Enter a keyword, and the Keyword Tool provides a huge handful of long-tail keyword opportunities, organized alphabetically.

Search Engine Watch

Search Engine Watch

The first place to start is with long-tail research and this can be done with the help of a number of tools. My first choice, however, is always KeywordTool.io.

Keyword Tool Helps You Find The Keywords That People Are Typing Into Google Search Box

Keyword Tool Is The Best Alternative To Google Keyword Planner And Other Keyword Research Tools

Here are a few reasons why:

- Free version of Keyword Tool generates up to 750+ long-tail keyword suggestions for every search term
- Unlike Keyword Planner or other tools, Keyword Tool is extremely reliable as it works 99.99% of the time
- You can use Keyword Tool absolutely for free, even without creating an account

Are you a business owner, online marketer or content creator? If so, most likely you would like more people to visit your website, read your content and buy your products or services. The easiest way to achieve it is to find out what your potential customers or readers are searching for on Google and create content on your website around these topics.

Every search is an expression of people's needs, wants, interests and desires. Imagine how your business would benefit if you could analyze search trends on Google, find search terms that are related to your business domain and customize content on your website to serve the actual needs of your customers.

Optimization has many subtle routes. Bot located optimizations may support deep rooting for lay authors. Optimization is also performed by Outbound marketing book sellers who manage bulk metadata for social sharing. Optimization also comes from cataloguing in library sites that store ISBN and ASIN.

In every email, campaign, link share and post, boost tags, keywords, hashtags and relevant links.

THE AUTHORS DEEP LEARNING

·The type of work
That optimizes your
Performance is Deep
Work."
Cal Newport

Deep Work is located in author's process and skillset. Machines can take this a step further into automation.

This refers to the author's process in learning. This is an intense process, involving cultivated neural rational skills. There is another deeper integration available. This is referred to as Deep Learning. Here the machine teaches and processes all variables and factors. Language translation on the internet is one of the systems of Deep Learning.

Digital Genius defines
"We train a deep neural network model by converting historical customer service transcripts into numerical representations called word vectors. We use statistical operations to extract meaning, context, and predict answers in any language."

Authors must step out of their comfort zone and participate in the disruption prevailing from digitization. Continuity from past experience and work flow that is conditioned, patterned and well styled, yet commands another challenge to be managed. This is a call for Deep Work. To access the full scope of the internet as a support than transcends all human brain limits and to command the many new tasks recommended is called Deep Learning. Consider being an author in English over a year to produce a book. It is a two minute task for the internet to translate into many languages and make it saleable across other linguistic regions. The author must continue to explore possible arrangements to provide leads and information that optimize his links continuously. He may promote through local promoters and advertisers. Advises books, for instance, promotes in Italy. Sakura publishing,

promotes in Japan. This is an Enterprise feature and the author must plan his outreach, campaign and collaborations.

Authors Intelligence from the core is assaulted in the race against the machine. New thresholds of performance, viral commercialization, productivity in new elite zones begins to manifest. The holocaust of paradigms, algorithms, work formulas and funnels must be programmed. Big Data must be contacted.

Operations are carefully guided. Authors must strive to access the blue print of the great cataclysmic change in session. Content remains king. The new buzz and development requires a new linguistic science of keywords and digitally programmed communication science. All this, according to Professor Cal Newport, brings elite styles of performance to routine work.

The author embraces the struggle for connectivity through the internet to develop his neurological capacity in focusing, and delivering a unified story despite the prevailing disruption. Focus, and concentration must meet with the internal space. The spiritual core also may be challenged. The internet has produced a revolution. To conquer the author must be well based in its key portals for metadata, analytics, inventories, competition environment, the judicial processes of the sites used, terms of agreement, of repair, of support, of feedback, and of continuity from past struggles. The author's livelihood is based on the internet, if books are not for free, or if in countries that do not support pre-paid books. The trends and revolution frequently and unpredictably move to destroy sustainability, crash good sites, control SEO externally or steal data, slow down royalties, retain funds or avoid confrontation.

The elite level of productivity emerges from the deep reading into the potential of the internet, strata's and specifications of Optimization, sophisticated campaign management and contacting of key Influencers. Insiders and experts must be located to boost the systems. To network the author must select professional, or paid portals, which may index, promote, sell, or fuel further discoverability.

Apps are available for enhanced design. What would have been

commissioned in artwork in days can be self-perfected in moments.

Quality in brands often displays itself silently. The author can arrange his own authors DNA, by managing profile descriptions and keywords to attract synergetic social and business development. A site as Smash words, can boost the author's exposure when located in a powerful network and selling technique. The author can own his own portal, and collaborate with similar groups, companies and locations, seeking similar work. A very exclusive author can set up Enterprise portals for a writer's guild or fraternity of elite producers. This involves heavy financial stake.

The scope of deep work is very great. This Chapter discusses the tip of the iceberg... simply so that authors train to manage their works and discipline in the challenged state. The author schedules his day to minimize distractions and reinforce control through sensory deprivation, avoidance of idle socialization and lifestyle commitments.

Facebook has already programmed internet users to maintain technical and compact use of elite emoji structures to remain social, engaging and communicative throughout the transition. This skill and feature is actually an arrangement that supports Bots at work, who depend intensively on feedback to grow. Authors may use Facebook to develop basics that will be needed more in other platforms later that promote performance. The way the internet is to behave for user's to score or benefit, will be noticed in Facebook as a primary destination.

Work agendas and work calendars must be focussed, prepared and skilled to meet with authors tasks.

"Instead of scheduling
the occasional break
from distraction so
you can focus, you
should instead schedule
the occasional break
from focus to give in to
distraction."
Cal Newport

Art belongs to Kynin Selm

AUTHORS STRATEGY FOR CHANGE MANAGEMENT

Authors are entering the era of automation, and machine based intelligence. They have to notice the change is contrary to their natural rhythms. Sometimes humanistic inputs are requested. Personalized stories has been recommended as a potential new style to develop a brand. The human voice incognito, through disguise and allegory is requested. The need to adapt and strategically address change in all activities, is obvious.

Brands are advised to impart humane intelligence to their product, as with biographies. Personal episodes and decisions that compelled change, personal styles and influences that spurred growth, and made an impact in markets. These are strengths authors are known to display. Authors have actively submitted interviews and personal stories to contribute to reader or fan awareness. In the age of automation authors will support the society by generating a human level to emote, react, connect, build relationships and maintain lifestyle so that the machine is not over empowering.

New process and revolution in automation, requires study of the change and its impact on authors lives. It requires investigation into the issues that compelled extreme organizational development in another dimension of robotics. The data to the sudden boost of Invention and reduction of originality, talent, creativity, small enterprise book release, is not available.

Let us hypothetically assume, that robotics, manages disaster prevention that is imminent, prevents bacteria and fungus that is epidemic, arranges big data for safe and secure controls that humanity evolves in a predictable environment.

Let us assume that the changes are expected to improve the situation in stages. Strategically managing the process flow should be within reach, and understanding of the supporting machinery should be with equalization.

These are technical difficulties that authors must handle. There is scope to discuss minor issues that impact change. The change from Publisher selling, to B2B marketplace selling, to B2C marketplace selling, increases the scope of sales over tenfold, increases scope of automated translations immediately on updated sites, increases visibility and discoverability of authors works also many fold.

At levels of social selling on channels as Twitter, sales have declined. Views are less in 2017 than 5 years ago. Author promotional schemes are less successful on Twitter platforms where maximum marketing is known. Facebook can be used for link sharing, emoji response, human interaction with technical competency, images sharing, app sharing, news sharing, invitation to events and available interactions on the internet that remain personable and social.

Instead sales may be better with blogs, radio broadcasts, video marketing, and book reviews, with advertisement campaigns, with comprehensive profile development, with community development alongside top Influencers, with expert Fiver gigs, with email marketing, with Amazon CPC strategies, PPC (pay per click marketing), app integration and specialized optimization for sales, lead campaigns, free days promotions, book giveaways, videos, launches, press releases or commissioned sales agents. Here we are still in B2B marketplace strategies.

Authors Enterprise is new and distinct. This is discussed at length later.

Appreciated in 2017 and beyond, are the technical communication systems, new keywords and hashtags, new whitepapers, new arrangements to study of automation. The author becomes aware that he is watched and data is configured around his performance. Emails, selling styles, personalization, up gradation to technical resources, performance in cloud and secure data transfer, uses of metadata and cataloguing. There is more care to the profile that is around the author's network, to sales rank, inventory, process, descriptions, back links and daily impact on the internet with comparative scores and analytics available. Authors own performance and improvement may be scaled. Arrangement to forms and emails are become complicated and include features of earlier website builders. Even Form downloads may have chats, voice recognition and AI. These may be active through CRM portals.

Authors can ask their leaders, platforms, guilds, community experts and critics to arrange charts, info graphics, white papers and technical guides so that their change strategy is quality assured, technical and adept. This will support the momentum into the machine age.

THE AUTHORS STANDARDIZED PROCESS

Here the core work of the Author is listed at level of the individual. The mean standard for authors remains consistent in its arrangement to self-publish, or hire professional support. This standard gives continuity to the past tradition. With added bonuses, bots and assistants as Amazons Alexa. Process must exist at the level of the individual, for it to grow to be an Enterprise and team later.

Workflow has become more supported, automated and stylized. Even for individual authors, not in teams. Content creation is a larger industry that is prioritized for developing technique, documentation, whitepapers, customer brochures, shareholders news and new business.

Brainstorming and aligning new concept for work, in secure workspaces is belonging to very different working process, apps and sites.

Authors immersed in their own data development, fiction or nonfiction writing, can take support of Artificial Intelligence. Slack offers bots that optimize and integrate. Bots also provides news and can give supportive information as publishers, latest trends on Amazon, security processes and indications of risk. The AddThis app can be integrated to share book links to favourite sites with coding and more to a vast social network of channels..

Without the deep structure and optimization according to guidelines, the book will no longer appear in search engines easily in the Marketplace.

The idea has not been to trouble authors and their work. The processes involved in change have belonged to billionaires. It has involved expensive satellites and robot labs to define arrangements in order that Big Data be obtained. It is not work belonging to the common man. Important working platforms are very expensive most of the time, and cater to Big Enterprise, where scaling and work process is defined.

Shareholders and funders lose control if they finance projects without data controls. Global information technology is essential for economic development.

However basic support from Amazon, Createspace and Goodreads continues as before.

PLAN
REVIEW
REVISE
DEVELOP
APPROVE
REVIEW
REVISE
SELF PUBLISH
PRICE
DISTRIBUTE
DESCRIBE
MARKET

The Authors processes are more or less standardized. Each stage covers essential tasks.

The PLAN stage requires a goal, subject, themes and purpose, readership and publisher. The genre and category are programmed An outline, description and engaging summary may be developed. In case there is a publisher, this may be submitted. In case it is self-publishing, the book can be previewed some weeks before, with a mention of expected date of release.

The second or REVIEW stage required checklists on the plan, date and objectives, and the appropriateness of the main text. Word proofing and editing may be automatically programmed.

The REVISE stage can invite external review of the manuscript outline, invitation of feedback, and development of revisions based on advice.

The DEVELOP stage may involve maximum time and focus to deliver a unified manuscript, with appropriate strategies, formats and techniques of language and style. The manuscript should match any announcement or approved book outline. The credits, quotes, dedication, back cover, authors biography and book cover should be included.

The APPROVE stage may be based on self-made assessment, approval from editor or publisher. It can also meet with automated checks from an internal digital technical editor that is programmed to pick up issues of bad margins, fonts, titles, images, page numbering, and spacing or related. Editing through internet based data sharing is not recommended except if the platform is very secure.

REVIEW in the post development stage involves managing issues related to the technical feedback of the programmed editor, or the manual feedback of the publishing team. Books get approved if technical standards, format, page size, colour and paper, margin descriptions or other formalities are correctly arranged, and compatible with the editor.

REVISE However tedious, especially for newcomers, chances are that revision will be needed. In new self-publishing platforms, new authors may require support of service professionals. Technical automated inbuilt editors can identify many issues, even if they are not manually noticed. Hopefully a service professional can recommend the best choice inn publishing specifications of your book based on your manuscript and preferences.

SELF PUBLISH your book on a known portal as Amazon, Lulu, Ingram Spark, Smash words, Draft2Digital, Kobo or personally owned and integrated portals. The book manuscript is loaded and converted for public sale and reading. Select eBook and paperbacks options. Fill up keywords and categories related to your book subject. Metadata is an important consideration for the authors intellectual stronghold to manifest in the digital landscape.

PRICE your book in all currencies available if publishing on Amazon, and in dollars in others. If you have a publisher, they will market on a B2B platform as Infibeam, Snap deal, Flip kart. New portals are in development to support the Internet of Things. However the link is generally connected to Amazon and must have relevant metadata as ISBN and ASIN. Fill up your US W8 tax form to receive payments for sales after tax deduction (15-30%). Note the percentage taken by the publisher apart from tax. Research the field or ask a Bot to research it for you. Find the best location for your work.

DISTRIBUTE based on options available in Amazons global distribution network on Create space for paperbacks, and submit your authors profile on Central in many languages to have visibility worldwide for eBooks and paperbacks.

Now the book is listed in the vast global B2B and B2C marketplace for sale, ranking, scanning, campaigning and related.

DESCRIBE your profile, your works, your stories, your videos, and your blogs in many engaging ways. Tasks change from authorship and self-publisher to seller. Locate critics, buyers and reviewers. Locate meeting places with common interests. Locate Self publisher promotional sites at discounted fees. Locate book critics that offer awards to bring authors into saleable spotlight.

For ENTERPRISE, locate a solution and CRM with comprehensive integration of apps for seamless workflow. This may include a purchase from KAPOST, from SCUBANA and SHIPSTATION, from a BITRIX.COM, AWEBER, CURATA, WORKATO, GETRESPONSE, UBERFLIP, APEX paid Intranet or any other amazing new arrangements which move books and authors in bulk via advanced website building platforms and any B2B or B2C Marketplace.

MARKET, via social channels, affiliate links, amazon seller services, stores, internet portals and options that emerge to boost your trade.

AUTHORS AGILE MARKETING

"An Agile approach enables you to become more effective without working more. You may get more done—or you may not. The point is that you're more likely to get the right things done."
– Andrea Fryrear, Chief Content Officer, Fox Content2

Agile is a new buzzword and system of workflow suitable for Enterprise based on altered and dynamic process. This Chapter is vital to understand the dynamics of change and productivity. Tools have been created. Individuals must mobilize them to maximum advantage. For example the *Paper bot* of Slack is arranged for default email, Facebook and twitter shares within working teams in Enterprise. Prior to 2017, the Enterprise would have belonged to documentation, legal standards, technical orientation and systems, many departments and intensive study. Now it is possible to ask a bot located for the Enterprise for support, locating images, files, and so forth. The Bot guides the employee simply. The support has been generated for the User specifically through AI. The user must develop skills to use this. For this reason tracking, feedback metrics and scaling is vital to the enterprise. Weak scores are backed by further support of AI(and more agile training.

Manifesto for Agile Software Development

We are uncovering better ways of developing software by doing it and helping others do it. Through this work we have come to value:
-Individuals and interactions over processes and tools.
Working software over comprehensive documentation.
Customer collaboration over contract negotiation
Responding to change over following a plan

That is, while there is value in the items on the right, we value the items on the left more.

The Agile Alliance: Mike Beedle. Arie van Bennekum. Martin Fowler. Jim Highsmith. Andrew Hunt. Ron Jeffries. Jon Kern. Brian Marick. Robert C Martin. Ken Schwaber. Jeff Sutherland. Dave Thomas.

The Authors Agile Marketing is needed by this time. Change has manifested in lifestyle, workspace, social media, internet and arrangements. What sold before does not sell anymore. Networks have changed. Previous connections may no longer have professional connectivity.

A new emerging strategy at this time is Agile marketing. Here systems involve rapid connectivity, adjustment, flow and delivery. The training is neural and absolute deep work with utmost focus. For example, the author may have to research new algorithms and processes that have altered the support nexus more formulas and support process. Algorithms refer to arrangements that alter the DNA of process and productivity. The author must align to new patterns for productivity and saleability that supports next level enterprise and scaling.

"Agile methods support rapid adaptation in a strategic, balanced way. ***Agile teams may be fast, but they aren't chaotic.*** *Choices are considered; decisions are not reactive."*
– Andrea Fry rear, Chief Content Officer, Fox Content6

Confluence of multiple and complex variables, as described with Ecosystems include convenience, mobility, agility, security and defined process characterizing the new era. The ecosystems of blogging, reviews, rating and marketing, selling, form around new algorithm inductions also which upset core learning. The author must be re-educated and agile to conform.

Known techniques for Agile marketing are SCRUM and SPRINT. These are core systems which support the re-education through definitive storyboards and planned assessments to survey performance in short bursts, goals delivered in less span of time than before, and team member support for improved productivity and adaptation. Some Start Ups offer Scrum training and agile skills for sellers.

More specifically Agile systems will suit authors as they belong to User stories, Themes and Epics to describe their PITCH. Scrum masters take over decisions on releasing products and converting stories for marketing.

A Theme example may be - *"I want to market a text book."*

An Epic may be - *"I want to market text books on the Internet to Corporates."*

User Stories may be - *"I want content standards for creating textbooks on the internet, and data on successful sales metrics."*

The central idea is groomed for sales performance and release of product development at home and in the marketplace. At Theme level the matter is simple. It involves developing a content pillar and text book and marketing it. The load and workflow systems are intense at level of User Stories as data and technical systems are put in place. Standards must be listed, textbooks outlines and verified, internet content matched, and scaling processed of prior successful development and corporate achievement.

An Author will develop his theme and story similarly, however with Agile it becomes an Enterprise feature, collective collaboration, unified targets and time managed controls for market scaling.

Details on the systems are provided from certified course trainers. The burden rests on the Author to ensure his sale. Skills training to the systems in hand must be capitalized for effective marketing. This preparation and reorientation is essential to embrace the larger developmental scenario and boost productivity in its confluence.

Quote (unknown author)

"Life is like Facebook.
People will like your problems and comment
but none will solve them,
because everyone is busy updating their own."

Hello reader? How are you today?

THE AUTHORS PROFILE

The Authors profile epitomizes his identity, genre, title, tagline and metadata. The author's new profile now must also optimize images, titles, statutes, awards, pricing, keywords, categories, location, personal biography, and influencer hashtag.

It is also the medium for search engines of the internet to recognize the true identity of the author, and decipher attempts to attack or impersonate through hackers, or register the presence of high ranked readers and influencers. The Author develops an automated dignity and rank based on the impressions of close community.

Intellectual property is the wealth and livelihood of the author. The internet has many means to maintain their dignity, data and professional security. Therefore the author should never compromise on fully developing their Authors profile.

In developing the author's profile, the author may choose his brand presence and decide on his goals. He must develop continuity in tone and persona, remain engaging and interesting. The authors profile must support CTA and clicks. The author must source new markets and convert audiences. The author must develop a deep system of integration, metadata and optimization on the new internet. The author may design integrated messenger branded bot chats, videos and shows. Established sites for metadata are Amazon authors page, Good reads, Universal Links, Draft2digital, Third scribe, Smash words, Create space, Windows live on outlook.com, Skype, Xing, LinkedIn, Anobii, Kindle Boards, Author on Amazon Central, KDP, Good reads, Word press (with RSS) and popular author platforms and blogs, updated for the changed Internet.

These are some to begin with. Ensure your email profile is fully established on Yandex Disk, Live mail, One drive, Box, Evernote, Dropbox or cloud based sites, Opera, Safari or other. Bookmarks in Instapaper, Pockets, Atavi, Pinterest amongst others supports SEO.

Manage optimized profile photo. Email leaks cause SEO to be stolen and vulnerability of fraud. Manage your key skills in keywords and hashtags to locate your area of the internet to be secure.

Manage optimized Facebook fan pages, group pages, carts, call to action, author landing pages, Instagram stories, Twitter profile and banner, Linkedin profile and author portal profiles.

The Internet is forming a digital footprint of all authors works, reading, influences, support, finances, skills, network, emotions, reactions and much more. The internet secures the authors status in comparison to others in the field.

This is also a career digital blueprint which moves forward if well portrayed.   The internet can also present others, colleagues, employees and competitors to the user based on the internal character reading.

In fact there are more advanced dynamics at work, as hologram configurations of author's real movements and activities which also convey the facts for controllers to recognize. These are discussed further in the last chapter.

AUTHORS BE SURE TO EMBRACE SOLOMO Social, Local Mobile
Ensure optimum outreach with own profile

THE AUTHORS NEW FACEBOOK

The authors industry canvasses across Facebook's feed to promote, share and engage. Facebook is the primary site for activation of the authors Amazon Central page and newly launched book, new Good reads review and all fans shares. It may not be the best selling place or buyers' market all the time, but it clearly supports the author's commercial rank and presence on the internet. We have it that Facebook controls a giant 40% of incoming traffic into the internet (e.g. login) and the distribution of data. This is more than any other single social channel. So far the impressions, emotions, social styles, intuitions and reactions of the internet community, expresses on Facebook.

Facebook is the first site that every new user learns on the Internet, and the first social digital community anyone has engaged. So Facebook also knows the common man best. Over the years, evidence has been gathered if the failing stability of the common man in his emotive intelligence and more. Political manoeuvres, election support, business support and community support were arranged. Later groups and individuals became spy and poking systems, to arrange alternate powerhouses. The dirty game, must have been assessed and a new update arranged in very powerful Algorithms, to allow Bots to capture the user's state of emotive and intuitive intelligence. This was coupled with the scope of activated bots to improve the user experience and arrange a social wellness level of convo (bot conversation) on the interface. This is an expensive paid feature and users should assess exact strength of action of developments. Testing is advised till the technical is understood in its impact. The amazing new algorithm has arranged many new systems for the Internet.

Social feeds and community is to become more responsible, creative and directed, and to obtain support via AI. Authors can develop and style their own messenger bot chats, introductions, sales, marketplace pointers and launches on their company pages through activating the Assistant support key and using a bot development site.

In fact Bots are to replace apps in their process of internet based AI support. This should engage users again and establish quality author brands. Moreover the newly featured Facebook stories provides authors with the attempt to brand their books and advertise. Facebook shifts from an entry point and distributing point to an able seller's marketplace. Facebook live stories also activates scope of live publicity and news making. The scope must be assessed and converted for successful brand sales through available guided descriptions, great words, quotes, design, images, stickers, styles and creative s suited for authors of all levels.

Augmented reality for Ed tech, F 8 developer's platforms, live streaming and 360 degree camera scanning suggests the new thrust of automation for all internet users and authors to build upon. Sometimes cookies may exist in emoji, which permits FB to access the users' data, computer, photo, profile, friends and activities for reasons of assessment and external social web control. It has already been suggested that prior evidence has necessitated extreme vigilance on the internet. The great number of fake accounts and automated likes, show past styles of spamming that may be cleansed at this time, as business, sales, elections and group movements were based on artificial tactics. Since FB is an important author's destination, it is best to move through branded solutions and discussions.

Facebook live stories also activates scope of live publicity and news making. The scope must be assessed and converted for successful brand sales through available guided descriptions, great words, quotes, design, images, stickers, styles and creative s suited for authors of all levels. The new algorithm has undermined the value of the Facebook 'like', in favour of the Emoji which is considered to show more engagement. So Emoji reactions count, not post likes. Updates on Facebook development sites as Augmented reality and 360 degree video live streaming from Facebook camera, provides remote Intelligence and great depth of information on the User or reporter.

However it may or may not collapse privacy seriously for users in ways some do not understand. To stabilize the users' loyalty, Mark Zuckerberg committed to increased WiFi connectivity for free for Facebook.

However loss of privacy continues to remain a sensitive issue. With use of Emoji, the science of sign language is international and covers stable communication amongst all races and languages. Emoji appears to be heavily based on cookies and deep learning neural networks on Facebook. Emoji's can be used to conceal students pictures, or it can be used to interpret colour preferences of the user and their personality types. The User should take care to follow if they prefer Emoji in Facebook or on Slack. Slack users will experience the powerful release of support on the internet based on bot feedback. Even Authors may enjoy Emoji's in there Facebook feed with loved ones, sick ones and children when they want to know there emotive state. Sometimes Emoji may be used as cookies from Facebook Intelligence. Facebook has offered the profile picture as a login feature. This may be useful and optimizing the photo. Login emails have been known to be hacked and mail boxes invaded. In fact the Facebook login mail id should be a less used one, or Authors should scan the barcode of the site with phone camera to ensure extra security. Yandex mail offers many levels of security when the site shows risk. Essentially, the new Facebook deep algorithms manages to structure emotional contagion, so that the wrong influences do not appear in the feed and wrong tendencies, reactions spread across the community. Facebook has also presented the internet's easiest CRM (customer relationship manager), for new advertisers that need smart office control in real-time. This is discussed in the last chapter titled Authors Enterprise.

The author must develop Facebook profile, fan page and Authors page adequately. Location, contact number, email, events, promotions, giveaways and much more can be listed for vast viewing. Promotions, stories, videos, notes, carts, shops, stores, follow ups, messaging and personalized marketing boosts are simple to amplify.

Optimization of Facebook images, headings, campaigns and launches also must be managed for distinction. Facebook's conversion tracking Pixel, must be managed on the retailers website in order to track conversions of visits to sales based on their ads. Facebook Product (book) catalogues must be synced with Pixel from Business Manager. Facebook's Dynamic Ads is closer to Authors Enterprise in scale than Facebook's static ads, and invites more conversion to sales. Dynamic ads is a CPC strategy in selling.

Further apps can be used to Segment, and encourage further conversions

*"If a site uses an on-site marketing platform (OMP) such as **AddShoppers** for their campaigns, demographic data can be used for multiple levels of segmentation and targeting. Targeting capabilities can be stratified using a three tiered funnel composed of segments, demographics, and personalization.*
Utilizing demographic data to efficiently target customers takes the form of knowing how to optimize your customer's journey."

"Using Facebook as the source for Refer-a-Friend campaigns not only captures data from the referrer, but also the referee. Even if one of the participants doesn't convert, their information is already captured through Facebook, further expanding your targeting reach. Facebook ads can then be used to target those customers based off their search history on the brand site."

From: The 2017 Guide to Facebook Dynamic Ads. Addshoppers + CPC Strategy

Image Optimization is recommended at least at 100 x 100 pixels. According to Facebook, Carousel format uses a square 1:1 aspect ratio images (600x600px) while single product ad uses 1.91:1 aspect ratio image (1200x 630px).

Use emoji often, and more than likes for deeper engagement. Authors styles and preferences form a digital potential support and scale also.

Below is the example of a typical Facebook page and Shop, which can be optimized through ads and campaigns, and quality books. The campaigns of these pages leave a deep impression which continues to boost and support the books visibility and impression on the internet.

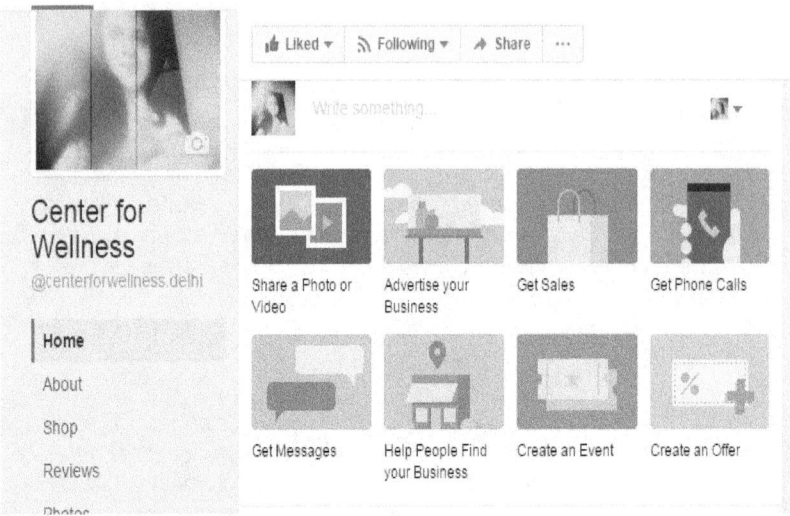

Call to Action must be well developed. Authors must decide on scope for conversion of traffic to sales, provide incentives and attract views. They can also combine with author groups, invite book reviews, feedback and comments, share video trailers, book launches.

The site should state Category, and Sub category, if it is an Author's page. Facebook promotions invite great SEO and conversion.
Facebook offers authors excellent benefits for one man show management with excellent standards of advertisement.
Facebook is also a great means of generating support, enhancing Authors image, following metrics and views and attracting loyal customers. Apps and promotions are well respected by Face books daily traffic.

Authors may invite agents and sellers to connect in a separate CTA if needed, or advertise for commissioned agents, collaborators and interested parties.

ACCELERATE MOBILE PERFORMANCE.
TAKE YOUR AUTHORS ENTERPRISE TO YOUR DEVICE

AUTHORS MOBILE USER EXPERIENCE AMPLIFIED

Author's integration with mobile platforms moves the system a stage further into IOT. Authors develop digital books for kindle and mobile devices to support the market read during breaks, subway rides, lunch, getaways and when travelling. Email marketing has to be accelerated through mobile open rates and 67% of opened emails belong to surfers on their device according to US Consumer Device preference report of 2015.

The author developing their brand to the mobile reader, may also follow rules of retention science, where words are few and captivating, i.e. approximately 6-10.

The Customer may be addressed at

Personal level (as with "you", 'yours', personal first name)

Emotional level (as with gains from discounts and giveaways, invitations to convert and optimize good feedback, retain customers) and

Popular level (as with cultural styles, genres, self-development support).
The youth of big metropolitan cities are trained to be engaged in good reading and locate time for their browsing. This pressure increases from schools and corporates, and from the changing momentum of enterprise.

Whereas older generations prefer paperbacks, new generation respond to eBooks. Student communities on the internet will require more support through mobile promotions, free chapters, support or related. Authors may prepare their own platform to integrate with apps for mobile fans, sell on Google Play, integrate with Facebook live video story promotions, and develop connectivity and support through several social channels, reviews, recommendations and referrals. They may arrange their books to be available through several mobile book e-reader apps.

Good quality videos and SMS marketing, promotions, should show the latest updates in social channels are fully used. Typography, GIF, Bots, messenger branded conversations and styles and exceptional image quality or style may be optimized.

The author may follow new trends for sales strategies as What's App marketing, Telegram, Instagram marketing with combined sharing to Twitter, Facebook, Tumblr and Flickr which accelerates views many fold.

Whereas security must be managed in mobiles extensively, many apps are available to generate support for Enterprise. Instagram marketing supports SEO and shares to several other social sites, if settings are managed.

SPECIALIZED APP SUPPORT EXAMPLE:

A particular App that deserves special mention is LeanPlum that offers key strategies for efficient ROI (Return of Investment).
Notes are delivered from Leanplum's whitepaper
The 6-Minute Guide to Mobile Marketing Automation

Key Strategy #1:
Gather Deep Customer Intelligence

Leanplum provides holistic personalization, creating deep user profiles that power relevant messages and optimized in-app experiences. Information grows and deepens over time, capturing attributes mobile marketers can leverage.

User Profile

Susan Liu

Email:	sliu@gmail.com	Total Occurences:	10 total purchases
Age:	25	Total Value:	$276 value
Gender:	Female	Device Model:	iPhone 6
City:	San Francisco	Push Enabled:	Yes
Country:	United States		
Language:	English		

Previous Time Spent in App — 3m 42s · Last Email — March 11, 2016 · Last Session — March 16, 2016 · Last Push — March 16, 2016 · Last Web Purchase — March 17, 2016 · Last Item Added to Cart — Ray Ban Sunglasses

Personalization Based on:

☑ Technology ☑ Lifecycle Stage ☑ Localization ☑ Demographic Information ☑ Behavioral Attributes ☑ Data Enrichment

This is rich data to segment and target push notifications, emails, and in-app messages designed to engage users, driving them toward key marketing milestones, add unique event parameters or targeting rules for each message, based on user profiles.
This automates and personalizes marketing efforts.

Leanplum suggests PUSH

"To successfully engage the greatest number of users, maximize push notifications opt-ins
On average, only 35 percent of users opt in to iOS push notifications. Increase your"opt-ins with Push Pre-Permissions, which suppresses the default iOS prompt and instead showcases the value of push when users are more engaged — for example, after they favourite a product.
Once you get their opt-in, you can engage users with push notifications that draw them back into the app time and time again."

Key Strategy #2:
Automate Timely Messages Based on Behavior

Start with transactional and service-level messages. With **Programmatic Delivery**, anyone can automatically send messages to segments based on key behaviors, in response to events like news updates, content releases, and promotions.
Linked data can be pulled in for added information on the user profile.

Key Strategy #3:
Coordinate Multi-Channel Campaigns

Use mobile marketing automation to:

• ***Onboard*** *new users with tutorials that help them understand the app*
• ***Engage*** *users with a series of content or promotions relevant to their interests*
• ***Encourage*** *booking or shopping conversions with cart abandonment campaigns*
• ***Reactivate*** *users with new app features or personalized deals*
• ***Persuade*** *users to submit App Store reviews or share your app across social media*

Authors attempting Enterprise level selling must utilize their mobile potential to acquire customers.

Remember that many others are competing in the race.

THE AUTHORS CUSTOMERS EXPERIENCE

Since March 2017, it has become time for authors to become serious about Customer experience. The scale of work is much bigger and the parts contributing to success, have become more sophisticated.

Customer centricity makes big sense when the social market scale is big. Some aspects of Customer centricity which commit to ideal situations include

: Scope for agents (analytics) to decipher the situation (marketability) rapidly, and arrange expert feedback

: Scope for more customer satisfaction at a better speed

: Scope for less calls and grievances.

: More trusted brands and customer loyalty

: Better SEO and site traffic

At this level of scaling, the internet has actively assessed the customers need, and purchase power. Social media and review support indicate scope for customer loyalty. The products (books) available are scaled and optimized to show up before the purchasing anonymous user.

Search engines can bring forward a hundred products (books), but SEO optimizes the most important ones to suit the customer. A search for Biographies, from a customer, generates a response of biographies, based on star rating, reviews, customers browsing history and preferences to surface on Page One of the browser.

In this marketplace, everybody cares. Social media, social support, social marketers and social innovators continue to develop the system and enhance customer experience.

Customers, at the same time, are empowered to help each other, through clicks purchases, comments, reviews, engagement, referrals, and updates.

The social commerce payoffs include
Relevance: 51% of customers like to share experiences
Outreach 1.5 Billion customers can access and interact with your brand anytime globally.

Conversion: The Marketplace has specialists who curate and review. These visitors are able to support conversion.

Innovation in the marketplace pays off with reduced time management, less risk and better customer satisfaction.

The Author can assess and plan for the customer personally by following the trend of questions and difficulties, and developing analytics for their preferred content. **Buzz sumo** is a site used for customer based social sharing data.

The Author may use the hashtag to develop his key brand based on a single keyword. Amazon is based on this strategy for its arrangement of brand interplay and customer loyalty. A single hashtag of Alternative medicine, provides focus and customer centricity to all visitors who have similar reading interested based on their collective digital impressions. The hashtag should be consistent and dignified. Spam hashtags reduce customer centricity and destroy the authors support. Remember to how up with key Influencer hashtags often so that their systems emerge closely.

The author can develop TYPEFORMS, to bring in customers ethically, so that they feel comfortable that they are not being spied on. **Type forms** may be linked to authors pages, email campaigns, landing pages, websites and blog shares. Type forms have strategic advanced specifications that manage the modern requirement of form building.

The Authors engagement with apps to Segment the customer is essential to compete with modern trends at levels of deeper engagement. An app called SEGMENT supports metrics in segmenting customers through demography, visits, reading patterns, spending patterns and personality patterns.

FACE TRACKER is an example of a modern app integrated with some CRM's to identify visitors to a shop. This is a typical experiment of Internet of Things in the new Ecosystem. The systems are invisible to most visitors, however Enterprise owners will show skills in similar research and metrics to obtain data on their customers. Facebook and Amazon are based on such tracking, if not the personal view, definitely the digital tracking is on record.

Face Tracker

Watch people visiting your brick and mortar locations.

✓ Face tracker uses face recognition technology to identify your clients. It can count all visitors to your store or your office, count how many visitors are new and how many are returning, and how many are in your CRM already.

✓ Face tracker can identify VK social profile by photo taken and add the profile to your CRM.

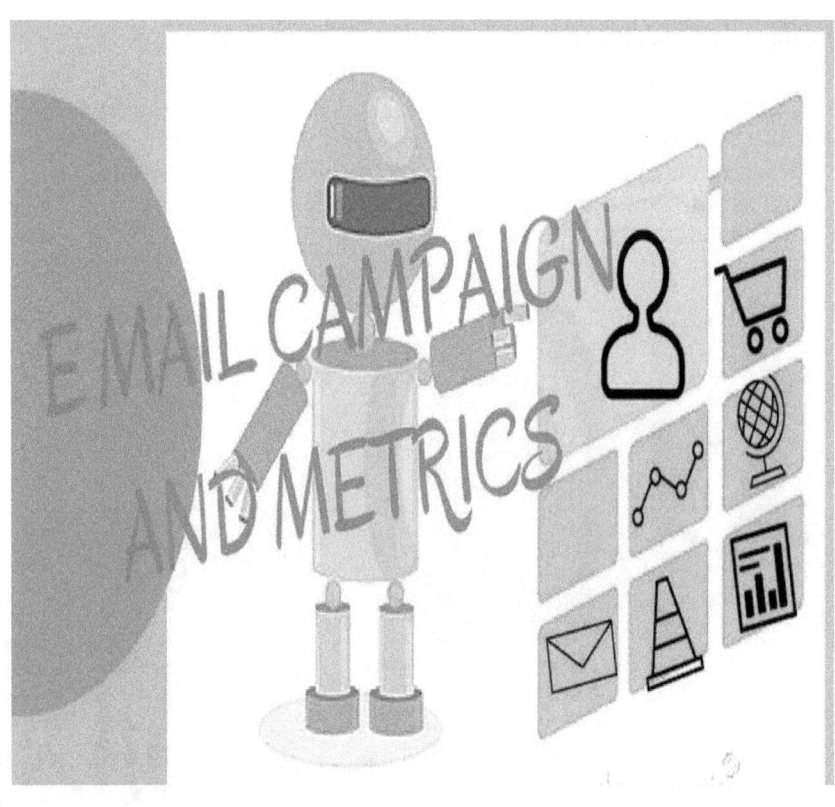

EMAIL MARKETING, CAMPAIGNS AND AUTOMATION FOR ENTERPRISE

Technical developments in the Internet have indicated preferential treatment will be available via email marketing for selling and acquiring customers. Many traditional websites are not being recognized by the internet. All sites are updated technically. New websites integrate features called for to optimize books, enterprise, websites, and brands and landing pages.

The email has become a very important tool for campaigning, selling, and developing customer conversion, retention and loyalty, especially for authors.

This arena of selling has been professionally developed through apps and integrations to cloud services for author enterprise levels where metrics and big data are needed. Individual authors can develop simpler professional styles through easier platforms, however personalized selling has been assessed to increase sales.

Email broadcasting/marketing/sms marketing, email campaign automation, and cookie transfer for customer tracking is included in the program. Scheduled shares, bulk shares, frequent shares and promotions as giveaways, gifts, buyer incentives, brand affiliations and more are some larger categories of email marketing.

Even these variations are minutely assessed and metrics obtained in Authors enterprise. Some integrations offer feedback and data for records, similar to Amazon Kindle inventory reports for authors. Some known and updated integrations amongst the recent launches include mailchimp, unisender, sendinblue, sendpulse, and campaignmanager. Campaign manager currently has upgrades that support integration with upto 250 apps for extremely advanced enterprise management. Social surfers will find many new growing additions and variations to email marketing. What used to be Word press or blog subscribers receiving new posts, with Mailchimp plugins and integrations to woo commerce, has graduated to personalized and detailed email marketing with many added features, including promotions, videos, webinars, courses, graphs, funnels, charts and chat supports which are private. The Campaigner has all the data in control of his Enterprise and one to one access to the customer, unlike social channels where many moderators preside. Also competitors do not interfere and process remains constant. Data without email marketing, is prone to aggressive hacking.

Geo-location and maps indicate remote markets that are responding to the Author. However active use of geo-location causes sensitivity of intrusion via satellite visibility which is sometimes unwanted and invasive. The use of augmented reality, Facebook live camera and similar systems in Snap chat, are not fully understood. They may be in use in danger zones, war zones or criminal pockets that need reporting. They may not suit authors.

ENTRY LEVEL

It is important to graduate and feel the market response and develop skills systematically.

The level of Individual, group or enterprise alters the workflow process.

At entry level campaigns may be via Canva templates, graphic designer templates or existing Microsoft Word templates. Below is a sample of a Canva banner.

Existing templates may be given a logo, message and picture. Links will be shared. However these are not with coding or in html. They must be clicked to be viewed.

Slack is a convenient workspace with Bots and secure sharing options that detects hackers. There are over two hundred apps for support of workflow and teams, internal communication, calendars, updates, development of tasks. Phone calls and video calls are also possible in Slack.

New Bot app integrations in Slack are very useful for unskilled users requiring support. Some favourites include Paperbot, MailClerk, Alertsy, Growbot and their offspring. Other apps unfold in the front page.

Samples of bot chats as the author has used it are below:

 PaperBot APP April 27th at 12:28 PM
in #general

Hey humans 🐺 nice to be added here too.
I organize all the links you share on
https://web.paperbot.ai.
I also send a digest by email, do you want a copy?

| Yes, daily | Yes, weekly |

👍 1 😊 1

5 replies

 malini 📷 6 days ago
Where can I share my links for optimization?
(edited)

 malini 📷 2 hours ago
http://ezinearticles.com/expert/Malini_Chaudhr
i/2388855

 malini 📷 2 hours ago
http://amazon.com/author/malinichaudhri

 **a** amazon.com
Malini Chaudhri

Hello Bot. why is my book not showing up

malini 🦝 12:16 PM
replied to a thread: Hello there 👋 you installed MailClark a short while ago. Are you happy ..

⟲ 1 reply

I am wondering why three books are not showing up

mailclark APP 12:50 PM
Hi, I'm Floriane from MailClark team 👋

Are your trying to send out these links by email?

🗨 Floriane Garde (MailClark Support Team)

malini 🦝 2:06 PM
I was hoping my links would be organized for the weekly digest.

But some are not opening here

mailclark APP 2:26 PM
You might be confusing bots, MailClark is a bot to send & receive emails, Twitter & Facebook messages without leaving Slack.

It doesn't organize links nor offer digest.

For digests, have a look at http://finalem.com/must-read. I hope it helps!

A bot to search for Giphys within the authors CRM

Giphy
This bot will help you find images matching your request.

+ Invite :Q

Monday, 1 May 2017

I can help you find images relevant to your request!
Type in something and I'll pick one for you! 😊

Like 5:30 pm

Robot images

Like 5:33 pm

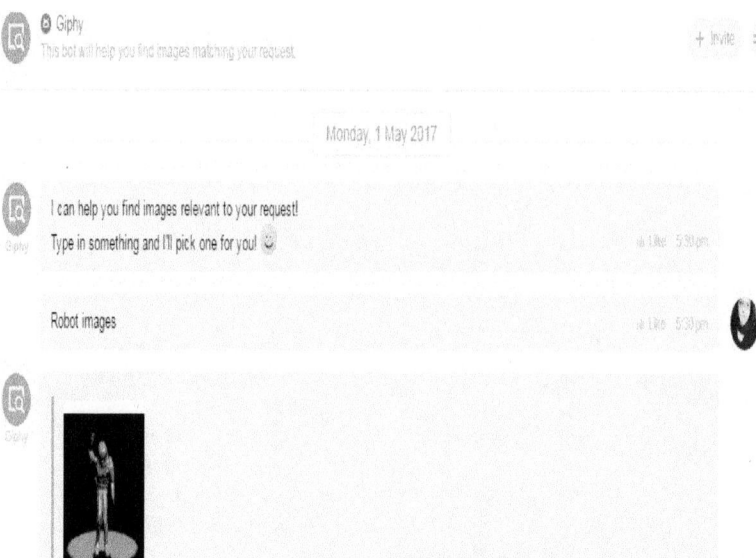

alertsy APP 12:32 PM
Let's get started! Type something you want me to search for...

If you need help at any time, just type `help`. To give feedback to Team Alertsy just type `feedback`.

Yesterday

 malini 5:35 PM
I want you to search for literary agents to sell my books on amazon

 alertsy APP 5:35 PM
I've added the alert. Here are team Center for Wellness's alerts.
The team can create **4** more alerts of which **0** may be custom.

> **Alertsy literary agents to sell my books on amazon**
> A Smart Alert created by Malini Chaudhri using the search term: literary
> agents to sell my books on amazon.
> **active subscribers**
> malini chaudhri

| Leave the channel | Delete channel | Customize alert |

When not with Artificial Intelligence or support of Bots, sites as Evernote premium offer scope for immensely popular free styles that generates a good impression and offers social sharing and mailing services with exceptional good quality and convenience. A campaign may be developed with scope for Headline, message body and picture template. It can be shared to Facebook, Twitter, LinkedIn, email or via link share to any social site. The Author can look at Evernote, for bypassing calendar and stop using calendars altogether. Evernote tags automatically generate a calendar for the user. Some authors with higher workflow and teamwork, may uses Evernote and its integrations with notes and notebooks, to build Folders for teams to follow. A tag WHITEPAPER, may help the team locate all documents and update at various departments of a single Enterprise, to locate relevant content and manage tasks allotted. This supports enterprise cataloguing at various levels. Evernote can be integrated with all essential Cloud CRM's. On its own, by connecting to the web app link, many handy apps for productivity, digital signature, developing workflow, and developing paperless company transactions to suit all needs

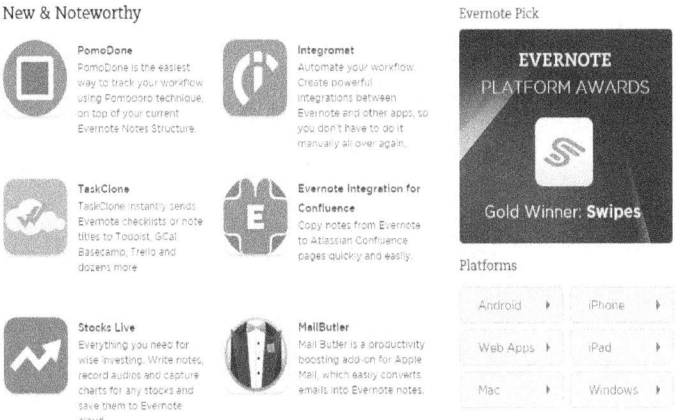

The network can be mailed individually without use of email in the connection, personalized share option. The campaign promotion can

also be used for social posts and links and images. These can be optimized through Bots if the author develops a preference for Artificial Intelligence and the link then shared on Twitter.

Dropbox paper and Dropbox for business are additional options for stylized marketing campaigns.
At all levels the neural networks are deep and it is necessary to tap the deep learning systems of the internet in its potential.

MID LEVEL

Here the User may prefer Mailchimp or similar integrations in Zoho CRM, Bitrix24.com CRM, Google Cloud, Amazon Web Services, Salesforce, SugarCRM, Vtiger, Highrise, Insightly, SuiteCRM Github, Zendesk or other cloud services. Integrations via apps may be available in hundreds. Very little is free. In case the author is able to design four or five free templates, these can be recycled. New apps are launched often with new features. Some websites integrate free email campaign features. Such websites are free or packaged.

CRM of Cloud secure services have integrated mail chimp and other inbuilt marketing systems. Most services are prepaid, and this is unsafe for credit cards which are fast tracked in the current scenario. The very little free support must be used by authors.
By now the author must have defined skills and targets from email marketing

TOP LEVEL

This is good for enterprise, bulk shares to large author's communities and networks with personalized introduction. The user must be skilled to the systems and follow team performance for optimum delivery and control. At this level the site can give information on recipient's re-shares, recipient's clicks to open, recipients conversion to purchases and the big data, which supports scaling and functionality. It supports large volumes of web traffic, funds and sales, publisher's listings, literary agents' activities, and book shops. It also enhances skills for future jobs and projects once the world moves to the next level of Internet of Everything.

The Author must ensure Quantification and Optimization of email activated workflow, enough that the enterprise identifies it as a responsive Push Channel for customer conversion and sales.

STAGES OF PROGRESS

*REACH THE INDECISIVE CUSTOMER
*ACT ON THEIR INTEREST
* CONVERT THEM TO LOYAL CUSTOMERS
* ENGAGE THEM FOR FURTHER SHARES, LIKES, REVIEWS AND SUPPORT

PRIMARY EMAIL MARKETING METRIC

Reasons for email marketing metric include:
* Increase in subscribers
* High-funnel engagement metrics such as opens or clicks
* Mid-funnel conversion metrics such as form-fills
(E.g. subscriptions, lead generation, inquiries.)
* Low-funnel conversion metrics such as revenue/sales/event
GET RESPONSE has indicated in a recent report that the need for segmentation and detailed overall email campaign efficacy. These can be used by Authors to scale Enterprise in the B2B marketplace and improve technical standardization. Standardized systems are needed for quality Assurance and Upgrades.

Type of segmentation used
>None
>Basic segmentation – we use 2-5 criteria for targeting, e.g. demographics, category of interest (B2C), industry, or role (B2B), without the use of dynamic content.

>We have segmentation, and also automated rules-based personalization for different audiences, E.g. using dynamic content.

>We use layered personalized targeting that
combines demographics with behavioural segments,
Lifecycle position, activity level, and lead

Authors should pay attention to segmentation as the significant lifestyle
component which generates potential of the reader, age, gender,
occupation, location, reading habits, preferred categories, extent of
engagement and the like.

Types of Email campaigns and notices may include:

Standard promotions and news
Promotional sales-focused campaign emails
Simple automated responders
Multi-step styled Bot chat welcome for new subscribers
Reactivation emails
Follow-up to cart-visits or clicks
Targeted lead generation

At any rate integration is to continue at a constant momentum and the
need of the hours for authors is to show AGILE

SCALING EMAIL MARKETING FOR SUCCESS VALUE

Assessment can be arranged for use of variations of
*Alternative Subject lines (Titles or Captions)
*Alternative offers or promos (discounts, incentives)
*Alternative email layouts and creative templates.
*Alternative landing page layout and creative.
*Performance by segment.
*Performance by frequency of emails.

Email marketing can also be combined with SMS and Telegram promos
for more mobile friendly engagement. Mobile messaging is not always
based on the internet. Systems can cover movements through mobile
data networks of communication. However this has to be assessed for
value as many find advertisements a bother and reject vendors with
such promos.

Currently the Internet is preferred as an ELITE system of communication and Information transfer. Images, colours and Fonts should meet with technical category for professional campaigning.

THE EMOTIONAL RATIONAL OF AUTHORS ENTERPRISE AND THE LOYAL READER

Diagram from GET RESONSE REPORT EMAIL MARKETING AUTOMATION EXCELLENCE 2017

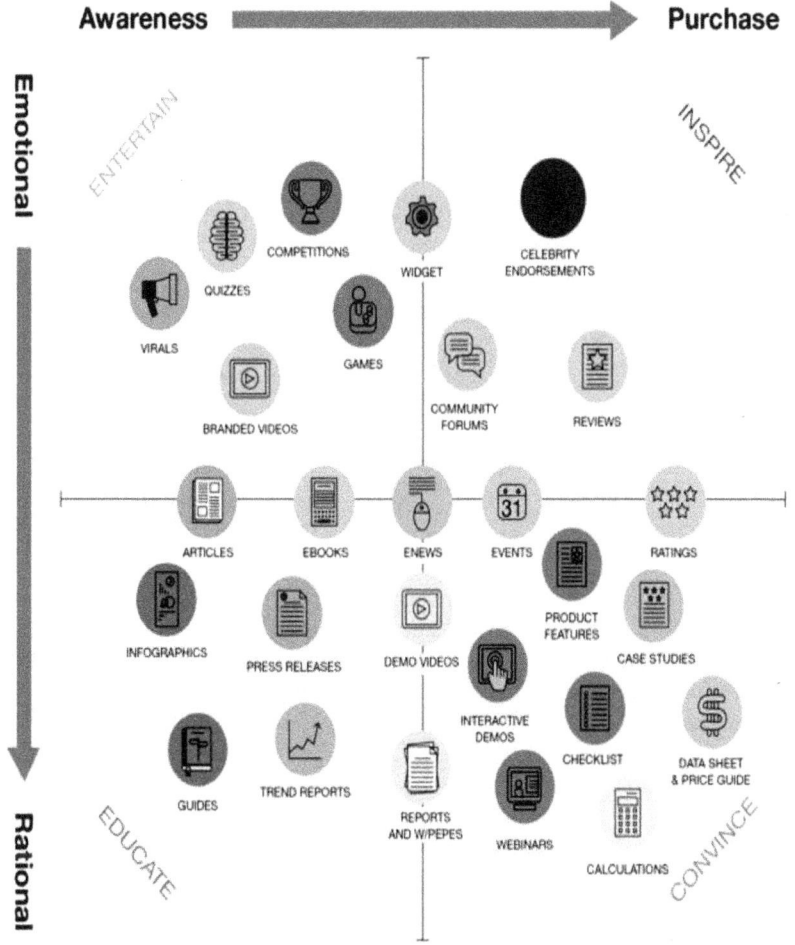

Marketing automation is a further step towards Enterprise and large scale selling.

Applications of marketing automation

Automated e mail marketing covers many stages of selling to a customer in the B2B marketplace which include

*Informing customer about new offers and promotions

*Informing subscribers about company news and new releases.

* Educating clients about the product and related topics through video/webinar.

*Asking for feedback and/or sourcing new ideas through survey, comments, likes, FB likes.

*Promoting other communication channels and social feeds. Inviting them to a Good reads giveaway or a free T Shirt on FB fan pages.

* Informing about transaction and other status. Status of delivery, availability, successful purchase, future rewards or more.

Marketing automation techniques currently being used are based on advanced integrations and sales management involve owning expensive and secret technical keys to access customer locations, browsing styles and spending styles on the internet that support techniques for conversion.

* Email automation.

* Basic profile-based targeting (standards of gender, buying category, book likes and reading profile, spending profile and related.)

* Personalization using dynamic content (also based on attracting target segments).

* Broadcast timing based on location, sign-up time or other criteria, as when the customer enters the marketplace or reads a book in the same listeria. This must be attempted subtly. It should not resemble watchdog or annoying styles of tracking that cause customers to report.

Advanced segmentation.

Here the Enterprise based seller must have adequate technical information about lifestyle statistics and patterns, sales probability forecasts and buying potential.

 Lead scoring. The Enterprise must generates adequate leads and conversions and show progress.

Content types distributed using marketing automation

Emails -facebook live stories- videos - webinars - bot chats-message series – blog posts- whitepapers – ebooks

Any or all of these automated systems support enterprise and contemporary corporate process in the marketplace since 2017. Examples may be found in DZone, Business to Community, Uberflip, MProfs, Get Response, Apex, Gartner, Scubana, Salesforce, Amazons app Webgility, Jungle Scout and many others.

Email Marketing basic terms:

Email marketing is a html activated marketing share system based on a template or drag and drop editor. There is a place for logo, image, heading, body, call to action, video (sometimes), chat box and footer with company link and address.

SMTP Server uses the reliable sever of a service provider as Send Pulse, using their tools and applications.

Webpush lets the author reach users when their customers or fans are surging the internet.

SMS Supporting messaging systems to subscribers offering discounts, new releases and more on mobile. This feature is available where internet is not available or for customers preferring mobile messaging.

API is for engineers who can support development of the system via tools available at deep machine level.

The most important advice for email marketing is to manifest a clear CTA and a unified tone to address the customer. Presentation should project the image desired for communication and retention. A bland email campaign loses support and is dismissed. Choose headers, captions, email subject lines, images, and layouts that are highly responsive.

PRODUCT OPTIMIZATION FOR AMAZON

Amazons optimization recommendations for authors have been provided in books, bestsellers and blogs in the past. Some of the essential information available covers Amazon kindle research tools and Category Selection.

Included in this selection are Support sites with tools listed below:
: http://salesrankexpress.com. Based on Aaron Shepard's Sales Rank Express

This site supports checks on Authors sales ranks, book monitoring and sales checklists. It provides basic data for optimization in Amazons book marketplace of print books, ebooks and audio books.

: http://ereaderiq.com. eReaderIQ offers price tracking service for kindle books and supports optimization based on pricing.

:http://kdpulse.com. KDPulse provides keen competitors support and advantage, earn about your competitors books and links, mainly to manage own book optimization. Negative behaviour as competitor gets noticed on the internet, so remain ethical.

:http://kdspy.com. KDSpy is a Google Chrome Intelligence service that Can assess kindle books, and generate support keywords for optimization.

:http://keywordinspector.com. Another Keyword Inspector based on your kindle books metadata. The ASIN number is tested for optimization and negative numbers of competitors is generated in European marketplaces for cutting into competition. It is called a reverse ASIN Keyword tool.

: http://kindlepreneur.com/amazonkdpsalesrankcalculator The kindlepreneur sales rank calculator is a free support tool to manage ranks and ratios of books sold per day for authors.

AUTHORS DIGITAL ENTERPRISE. MALINI CHAUDHRI Ph.D

http://kindlesamurai.net . The Kindle Samurai assesses the scope of author's keywords and the placement of the link in the front page of the web.

http://klytics.com K Lytics is a tool and market leader that provides data and information on the market, authors, sales, and trends that enable adaptive marketing from sellers.

http://merchantwords.com MerchantWords is a data scrutinizer that lifts the most wanted, or browsed keywords for books in recent days. This can be used by authors.

http://novelrank.com NovelRank is a book sales tracker that provides information on book sales and relevant data to browsers of Amazon books.

OPTIMIZATION

SCUBANA has indicated listings relevant to Amazon sellers after March 2017 where the standards of optimization grew even stricter. These may be followed by authors on the author's page at Amazon Central.

1. OPTIMIZATION GUIDE FOR VISUALLY CAPTIVATING PRODUCT TITLE AND LISTING

This optimization recommendation suggests that the title is the main magnet that pulls the customer in from the search engine. It should be compact and contain an influential keyword. The keyword should appear again in the sub title, body of the description and in tags. Keywords indicate the authors' area of skill and competency. Keywords may be listed on Kindle or Create space when submitting the book. Popular keywords as Non Fiction, DIY(Do it Yourself) or Self

Improvement, attract sales and have repeat reading value. Listings and titles should remain consistent on authors book blogs, Goodreads tags, Createspace tags and Cataloguing sites.

2. OPTIMIZATION GUIDE FOR PHOTOS

Photos and images are essential factors that attract sales. Images should be clear, uncluttered and show details of the product. The primary image should be 1000 X 1000 pixels with high resolution and good quality. The marketplace has zoom features and the image must not blur in the search. Amazon accepts JPEG (.jpg), TIFF (tif), or GIF (.gif) file formats. JPEG is preferred. Eight more images are allowed on the author profile page on Amazon Central. These images can be managed for attracting readers to the site.
The book cover editor advises the author on the resolution needed for a perfect cover.

3. OPTIMIZATION GUIDE FOR PERSUASIVE PRODUCT DESCRIPTION

Product description must be technical, persuasive and compelling. The authors' language should indicate his level and the style of the book. The author can insert keywords, influencers, and range in his description if it supports the sale, and also present the book as newsworthy. If a storybook, the plot should attract. The authors' biography should be well developed along with a profile picture that may be optimized and recognized on the internet.

4. OPTIMIZATION GUIDE FOR POSITIVE PRODUCT REVIEWS

Five or four star reviews are essential for book sales to move. The author can approach professionals with ethical arrangements to review. Amazon's algorithm filters out negative reviews, which tarnishes the product. All buyers are given follow up mails inviting book reviews from Amazon. Facebook has Kindle groups involved in review exchanges. Examples of reviews Amazon does not allow are listed below. The Seller becomes unethical in Internet ranked scores:

* *A product brand posts a review of their own product*

A customer posts a review in exchange for cash, a free or discounted product, a gift certificate, or a discount off a future purchase provided by a third party

A customer posts a review in exchange for entry into a contest or sweepstakes or membership in a program

A customer posts a review of a game in exchange for bonus in-game content or credits

A relative, close friend, business associate, or employee of the product creator posts a review to help boost sales

A customer posts a review of the product after being promised a refund in exchange for the review

A seller posts negative reviews about a competitor's product

An author posts a positive review about a peer's book in exchange for receiving a positive review from the peer

5. OPTIMIZATION GUIDE FOR COMPETITIVE PRICING

Pricing should be systematic and lend with other sellers on the marketplace. Authors price their books based on the level of profile, or on the readers market and their financial arrangements. Science books are expensive and buyers maintain budgets for new books. Romances are easily finished and may be cheaper for kindle readers and big traffic. Under pricing is not recommended. The author develops his market potential and career in the marketplace.

6. OPTIMIZATION GUIDE FOR SEARCH TERMS AND KEYWORDS

Search terms and keywords have been discussed widely, but here it is important to follow that visibility and authors' ranks are influenced by the keywords. Links can be tested for scores in sites as scrubtheweb.com or elsewhere, which provides feedback on site performance.

7. OPTIMIZATION GUIDE FOR ADDED MILEAGE AND PAY PER CLICK

Authors can opt for sponsored advertisement campaigns for their product as arranged in the pay per click option. The author sees clicks and pays for the campaign to be active to the customer. Clicks in the marketplace optimize the product.

8. OPTIMIZATION GUIDE FOR PACKAGED SALES (MULTIPLE ITEMS DISCOUNTED)

Recently Amazon provided arrangements for packaged sales. A book can be sold with a gift. Alternatively several books may be packaged for more sales.

Amazon continues to evolve and new high tech apps for professionals are available for optimization and testing. Splitly boasts below:

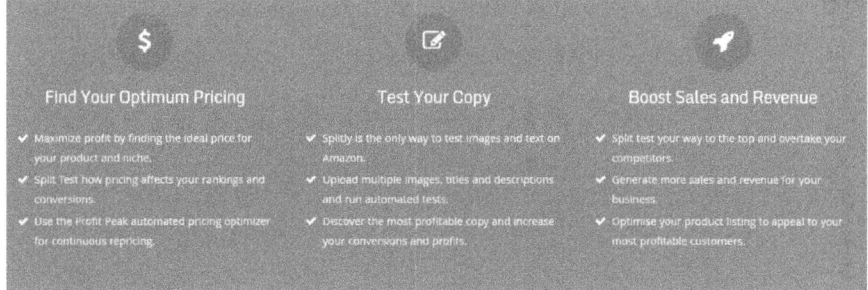

Fetcher is another important Amazon app essential for Digital Enterprise

 FETCHER

PRICING   ABOUT US   BLOG   LOG IN   SIGN UP

1. We Fetch your data

2. Our software runs the calculations

3. You get your finance stats

It only takes 1 minute to sync your Amazon account – after that, we'll automatically import all historical data.

Fetcher calculates your business critical metrics like profit, PPC, refunds, fees and more – updated every minute.

Rest easy – your accurate financial metrics are at your fingertips helping you make better business decisions.

93% of customers say Fetcher is *essential* for running their Amazon business.

SCALING AUTHORS ENTERPRISE

The pace of development continues to overtake Authors. Digital Enterprise is a relatively challenging arrangement to configure for those interested in joining the race. It requires new skills and adept practises in company work, tracking of web and real traffic, new developments, apps, content marketing and management systems and Customer Relationship management via portals.

There are two systems of marketing. Inbound and Outbound.

Inbound marketing has consistently provided maximum mileage and returns on advertisement capital.

1) **Outbound marketing** is expensive, pays advertising professionals, freelancers, booksellers, book promoters, book agents, publishers and literary critics to move the market. Authors may have access to institutions, traders, and vast libraries for arranging sales.

2)   **Inbound marketing** provides scope for intensive management and control through data analysis. It provides secure inventories and evidence based enterprise which may be protected by Law in case of infringement or breach of contracts. Social planning and investments, scheduled tweets, combined social shares from a CRM, tracking, conversion metrics, visitor engagement, email template design, and campaign, email list building, paid social advertisements in own fan pages, building of reader groups, inviting re-shares, personalizing readers engagement and reviews. The Enterprise develops its brand, picture styles, captions, fonts, language and CTA consistently, daily and with Time Management, and daily reports. The nature of the Enterprise, the budgets, the scale involved, alters the workflow process and CRM usage.

Revenue has to be the mother of all metrics. It's what we're here for, right? "
—Doug Kessler, Creative

Director/Co-Founder, Velocity

In all of it the ROI (Return on Investment) must be calculated to shows the returns on funds spent. To do this Production cost metrics and distribution cost metrics, along with lead metrics and associated financial metrics must be interpreted.

ROI (C) = Σ
$ Revenue generated by x
($ Production cost of x + Distribution cost of x)

From Curata Metrics Ebook

Digital Authors Enterprise is now the system. The individual author may get lost in the maze. The Internet values a strong stamp and blueprint which contributes to the Big Data. The controls and interests belong to Shareholders, Billionaires, Top management, and experts who have overall control of the scale with scope for predictive analysis. The market does not favour experiments or losses. They require instant feedback from the programs on the internet which measure success and failure. The world gets systematized every day.

The role of Amazon in the Scaling is very impactful. To understand Amazon is to follow their contribution through apps that support entrepreneurs assess the breakup, the trends, the top marketers, the most browsed keywords, the competition, and the arrangements of the marketplace that supports enterprise to perform financially. The Enterprise must show the ability to process information and metrics of the field in order to feature. The aim of this chapter is to move into the popular systems available on the internet, before they manage Amazon apps. The key concepts and dynamics of complex marketing should be followed first. Amazon comes last in the priority list of research.

1) FACEBOOK

First comes Facebook. Every basic system is available to manage on Facebook. The complex funnel of the advertisement from the small scale entrepreneur can be administered and designed at home. The units described are greatly targeted and assessed by marketing experts in large enterprises. The initial systems and styles fall into place till the seller graduates in skills and technology.

This approach is known as Full-Funnel Conversion Rate Optimization

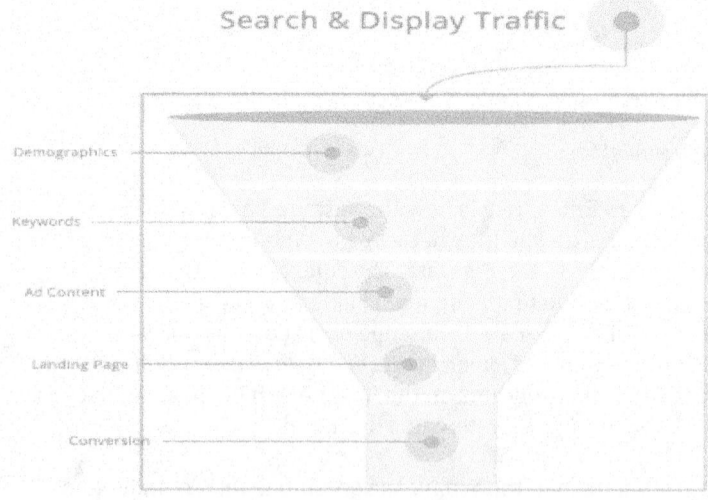

Remember: In order to optimize for the full funnel, you'll need to map out the entire user journey, and test multiple variables at each stage of the buying process.

Here is an example of a full funnel approach for a B2B company.

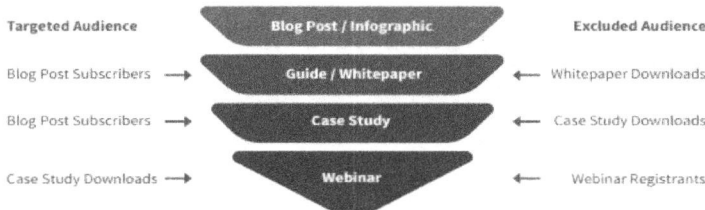

In this example, demo/webinar registrants are considered "sales-ready" leads and generally move from marketing to sales at that point. For each stage of this funnel, the advertiser can run post-click campaigns to address the drop-off at each stage.

Figures above are from :*How to Perform Full Funnel Conversion Rate Optimization.* Optimizing Your Audience Targeting, Ad Content, Landing Page, and Post-Click Experience

The simple systems can be mastered until scores are improved and sales or reactions are visible. If the results are positive, move further into the System.

2) CRM

CRM's and app integrations, communication systems with tracking and detailed company management tools support the next level for Enterprise.

Locate templates with formats to feed your idea into crowd funders. The role of finance is crucial to manage enterprise as investors, banks and consultants ensure the journey is smooth and the systems are intact. A template from Kapost is below for content marketers pitching their ideas.

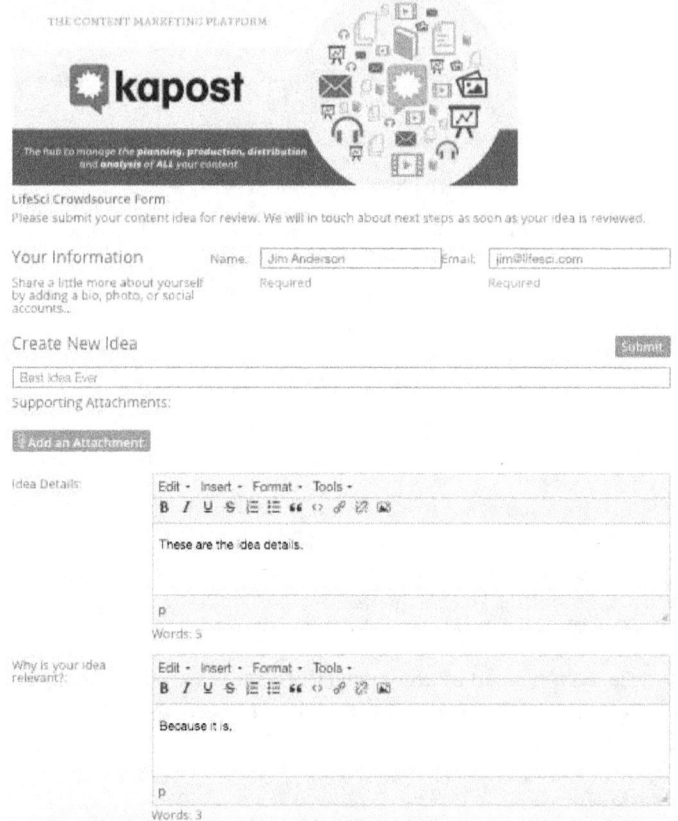

More from basic CRM styles with app integrations. This range is from an elementary free intranet and integrated CRM

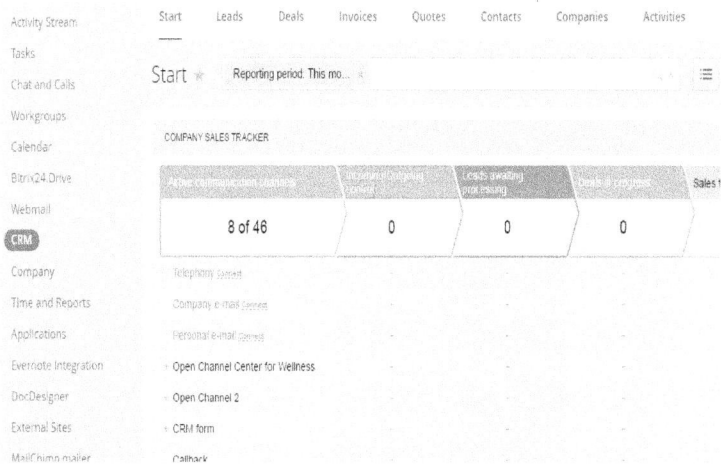

Note the progression from the Facebook elementary system of sales funnel to a comprehensive system of data management.

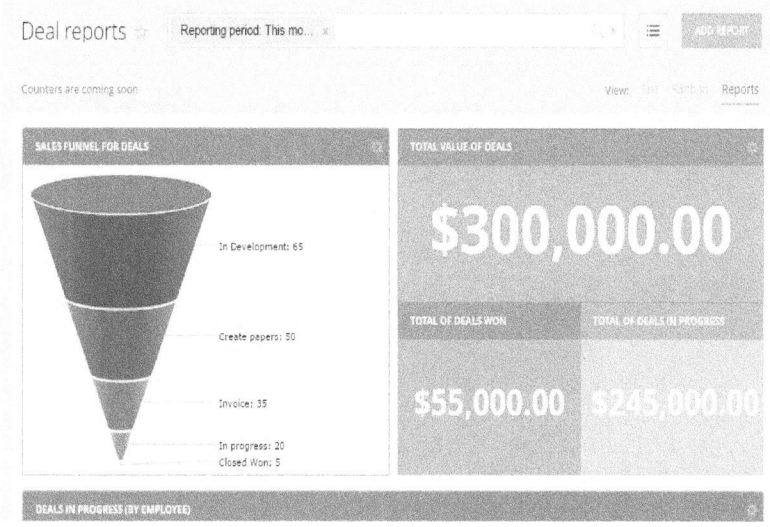

The Hyper script integration allows the AI to interpret the customer s call and script it. It also assesses calls to interpret reasons for loss of customer. It supports scaling of improved sales based on feedback and correction of conversational mistakes.

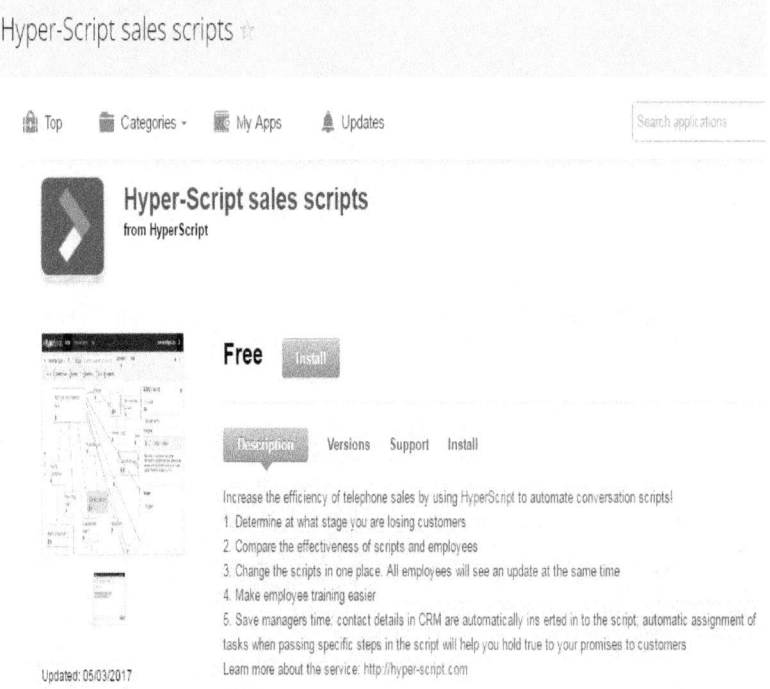

Below, the Roistat app integration works as a keyword tool that supports locating the best keywords to optimize the business, and interpret data across many business. It can support accurate forecasts of profitability. This app resembles Amazon's Splitly app, which is designed mainly for Amazon sellers.

94

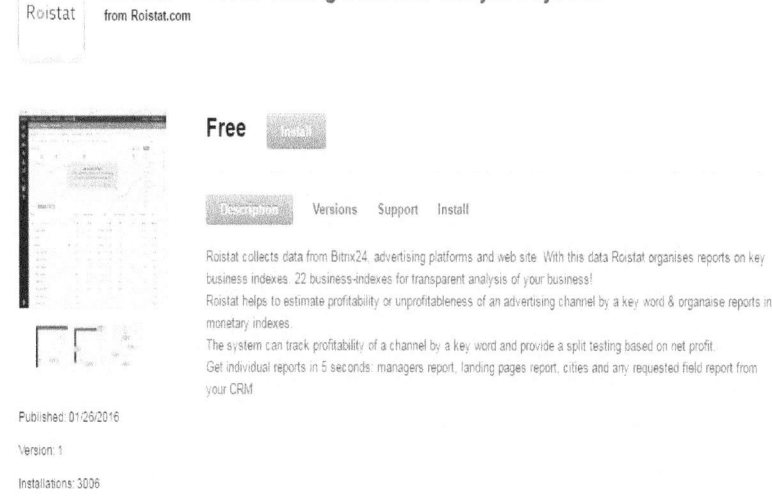

CRM"s are vast and varied. Many should be tested for convenience.

3) Slack Enterprise Grid

Slack Enterprise Grid comes with 900 potential app integrations and added security. The previous mentions of Slack in this book are taking ahead and assembled with vast potential for empowering workforce.

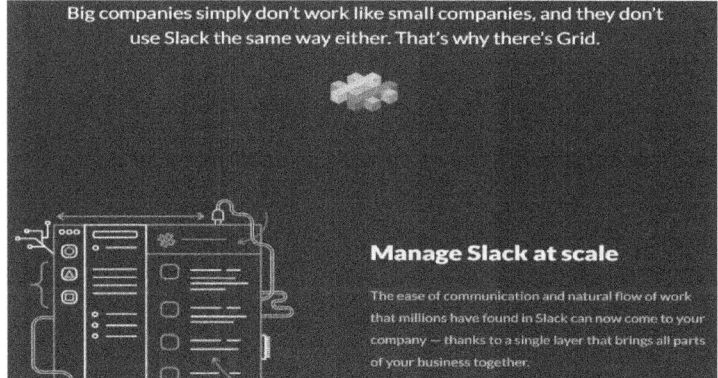

Slack is the most popular connector for work teams with Bot support and AI. Security of content, of co-authors and editors, of teams and colleagues is managed along with exception phone and video support, screen sharing, conferencing, and next level enterprise support.

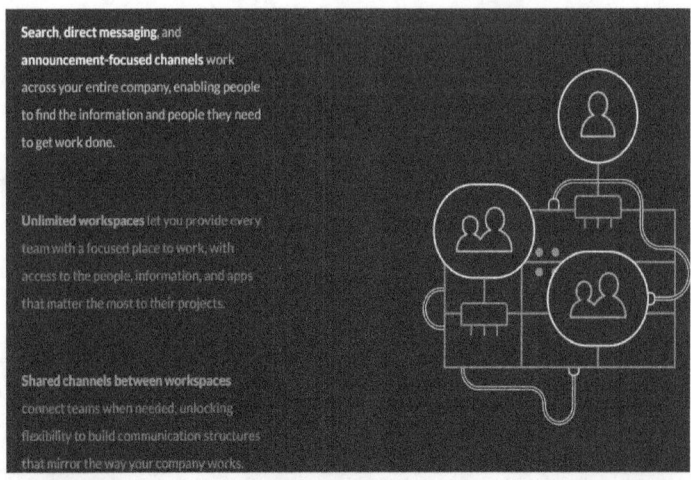

4) **Zoho Social**

Zoho Social is a smart social extension to some browsers, and part of the ZOHO system which is integrated with with email campaigns, website builder, CRM and more.

This social dashboard supports daily posts, web traffic, scores, optimization and records in a beautiful new template. Twitter messages and Facebook fan messages reach this site Metrics for daily assessment of traffic and engagement from posts shared to several social sites from one dashboard. The feedback and scale looks more encouraging than that of a simple Facebook post. The display panel provided excellent support for inbound marketers needing scheduled, automated execution and management from the browser, mobile or during travel. The strength of Big Data analytics is secure more than other sites which can be hacked.

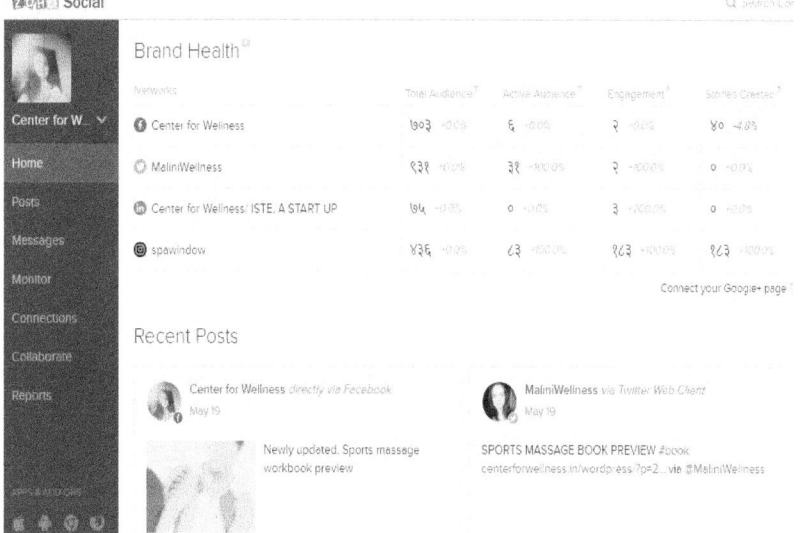

is one such example. Many marketing portals exist for inbound practises

5) Arrive at Inbound marketing in Hubspot and Github, Workato, Zendesk, market, Curata and others

A Zendesk Call Center image is below

Make the call

Zendesk Talk is a web-based call centre. No more messy hardware, fumbled calls, or bad hold music.

Spark the conversation

Zendesk Chat instantly connects you to website visitors through real-time communication and powerful user intelligence.

Be there 24/7

Zendesk Guide curates knowledge for your customers and your agents, so everyone can find the answer they're looking for, wherever they are.

New Chat Contacts

Product Usage   New Messages

Conference Leads

DROPBOX   **INTERCOM**

EVENTBRITE

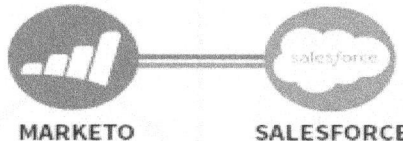

MARKETO   **SALESFORCE**

Triage

Review   New Lead Alert

Enrichment   New Qualified Lead Alert

Product Usage   Upsell Qualified Lead Alert

*360° view across
Salesforce,
Intercom,
Eventbrite*

   +

SLACK   **WORKBOT**

Marketing Workflow Automation in Action – H2O.ai

From Slack's H2O.ai

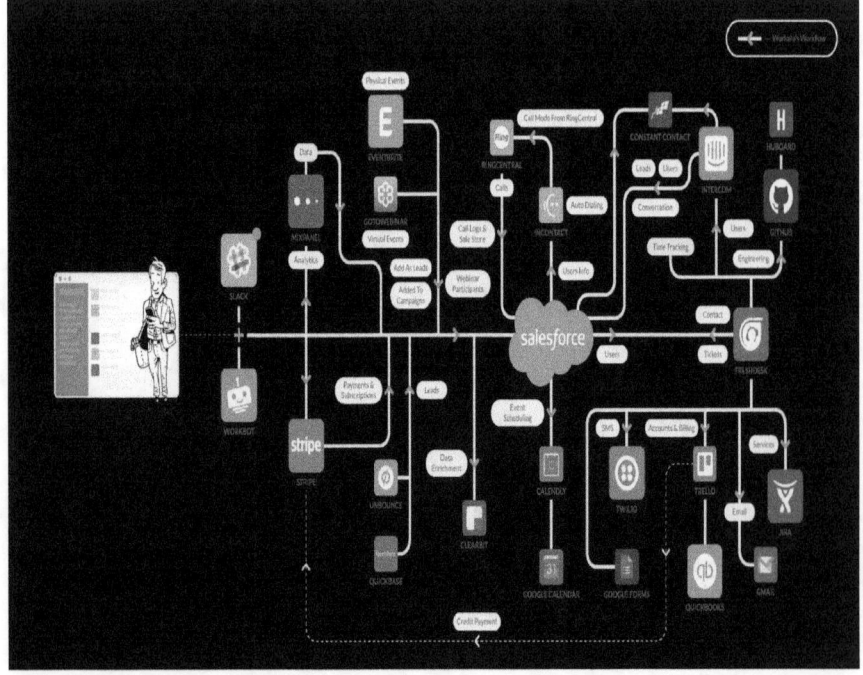

Workato sales leads comes 17 different cloud apps that gather leads, manage customers and store information.

Workatos advise for digital transformation:

Must be both enterprise grade and operate at consumer scale

Integrations and automations are not just built-to-last but also built-for-change

Must empower specialists and IT as well as LOBs, citizen coders and digital employees

Powerful yet 10X faster deployment and iteration of integration and automation projects

Auto-Scalable, Always-on and Zero devops. Users should not have to deal with peak loads, provisioning, high availability, fault tolerance, versioning of recipes, system upgrades

Always-on like a utility and a dramatically (10X) lower TCO

AS presented in Inside Workatos Kitchen whitepaper

5) **AMAZON**

Manage your Enterprise skills and systems then reach out for Amazon Apps, or sister concerns for added scaling. Explore possibilities of Amazons new ventures, new releases, developmental schemes, Alexa skills and make it all come together.

Amazons **Webgilty** advises in Cure *for Ecommerce Chaos Whitepaper*

"Follow this handy set of instructions by choosing best-of-breed applications that work seamlessly together and you're guaranteed to get a pulse on your business's financial health, understand your markets, and know how much you're making on a particular order or product. Eventually you will know if your customers are coming back and why. And because a single, accurate set of data will be seamlessly coursing through all applications, you'll have spare energy to bolster your e-commerce immune system and even enjoy a great night's sleep. "

"1) *Margin cure: Add test channels. To keep it simple, choose a single product to sell on Amazon. Use that space to experiment with promotions and margins—with just a few quick clicks, it's possible to increase sales by 50%. "*

"**2)** *Long term traffic remedy: It's never too early to prep for the holidays. If you're thinking about driving sales during November and December, then you're too late. On the flip side, it's never too early to start ensuring that your customers will come back to buy again, so January is a great time to work on customer loyalty with a series of engaging welcome emails."*
"3) *Sellers who think about the big picture instead of just focusing on getting through the busy season see a huge increase in return*

"Organize inventory by alphabetical order, *style number, brand, location, and however it makes sense for you and your fulfillment team."*shoppers."

" *4) Data Automation* is the process of instantly connecting and syncing all sales data to and from your sales channels, accounting, inventory, and shipping systems, ensuring that you can operate your business from one timely and accurate system of record. Because downtime from changing or improving systems means low—or no— revenue, data chaos ensues when a seller's chosen systems and platforms are not compatible. "

"5) Inventry and Warehouse Management Systems take care of everything from demand planning and forecasting all the way through to the fulfilment process, usually on the cloud. Large, complex inventories cause a lot of chaos, so sellers need to make sure their SKUs, prices, and quantities are always reflected accurately on all platforms."

Webgility

AUTHORS DIGITAL ENTERPRISE.   MAINI CHAUDHRI